CHANGE OR GO BROKE

STRAIGHT TALK ABOUT SMALL BUSINESS

Ken Hail

12/09

CHANGE OR GO BROKE

Straight Talk About Small Business

Kevin Hanville

LANGDON STREET PRESS
MINNEAPOLIS

TABLE OF CONTENTS

SECTION IV EMPLOYEES

INTRODUCTION

I don't care to belong to any club that will have me as a member.
~ Groucho Marx

Fair warning, I pretty much say what I think and I am not concerned about being politically correct (to the extent that it keeps me out of lawsuits). If you take straight talk as insensitive or mean, don't read this book. Before you go firing off a blistering email or review because you are taking what I am saying personally or you don't like my "tone" – either put the book down now or get used to it. If after this warning you still read this book and are offended to the point of writing me an email, note that I will probably not read it. I consider those types of indignant outcries as similar to complaints about the noise from someone who decides to move next to an airport.

Here is a little about me so you know who your driver is on this politically incorrect journey. I am not from academia, spouting a theory about small business that sounds great in a classroom. I've "been there" when it comes to small business. I *have* sometimes had to make payroll with my American Express card. I have been knocked down and got back up, again. The cycle always repeats. I am an entrepreneur at heart. I am a bad employee. I am not some twenty-five-year-old kid who made millions in the dot.com era (although I tried) and now thinks he understands business and life and is going to enlighten some fifty-year-old with his wisdom. Wisdom is earned and experienced.

I am not a "kumbaya" kind of guy and this is not a "kumbaya" kind of book. I don't subscribe to the notion that we all sit around and "think" a great business into being. I have seen plenty of people "think" themselves right into bankruptcy. I believe in actually doing something instead of sitting around talking about doing something, and then feeling good about ourselves because we "tried."

I think a major goal in life should be to try to not do stupid things. And when you do, try not to do the same stupid thing more than once. The more I learn, the more I realize how much I don't know. Have I made mistakes? You bet, tons of them. Pretty much ruled me out of running for public office...

This book reflects my style and beliefs as a business consultant, executive, and business owner. If you are familiar with the DiSC psychological inventories, I am a very high double "D." If you are not familiar with the DiSC system, suffice it to say that I am very direct and to the point. I was born with a personality "disorder" where I say what I think (this is one of the reasons I am no longer in corporate America).

A good friend of mine is author Michael Leahy who wrote *Porn Nation*. He said the readers of my book need to know who I am. So, he described my personality (it is kind of unsettling when somebody nails you this accurately). He said I am: "surprisingly frank, unapologetic, bold, in-your-face, matter-of-fact, confident, a guy who rubs a lot of people the wrong way, definitely NOT PC, opinionated. If you were a fireman on a ladder leaning up against the window of a burning building, and you were talking to someone inside who's about to die if they don't take your hand and get on the ladder with you, I'd envision you as calmly but sternly saying, 'Listen, you've got two options here and not a lot of time. Either grab my hand and climb down this ladder with me, or get ready to die. It's that simple.' Not callous, just telling it like it is."

For some, I am the fireman on the ladder.

I have worked my entire life – no silver spoon here. The following timeline pretty much describes my working career starting in elementary school (roughly in this order): paper route, Dairy Queen, grocery store, pizza delivery, bartender, restaurant manager, corporate sales rep slug, entrepreneur, corporate national sales manager slug, entrepreneur, corporate VP of sales slug, franchise owner, business coach, public speaker and business consultant. Yeah, I get bored about every three years or so...

I have the utmost respect for the small business owner, especially since I am one. In corporate America you can make a mistake and it may only cause a ripple for the company (unless you were a CEO at Fannie Mae and Freddie Mac). But make a similar mistake as a small business owner and families lose their livelihood.

I believe that life does not have to be hard. Yet, most of us make it harder than it has to be. I believe that life is not fair and far more random that we would like to believe. And I believe we need to stop taking ourselves so seriously.

I remember being in a company meeting when I was a VP of sales. We were discussing the current state of one of our software products. Sales, marketing, development, and professional services departments were all represented and everybody's positions were pretty well dug in. The meeting was starting to turn into a heated debate. About the time my head was ready to explode from the inane banter, I interjected something intended to lighten the mood. I said something to the effect of: "Lighten up everybody, we're not curing cancer; we are only writing software..." Cue the crickets... If it was proper corporate etiquette for the mob to stand up and start yelling, "Witch! Heresy!" – I would have been run out to the parking lot and strung up. I was reminded of the scene in *Monty Python and the Holy Grail* where the crowd was chanting, "She's a witch! She's a witch!" I was living in a Dilbert cartoon.

We need to laugh at ourselves and life around us. My son says that I laugh at everything. I don't have the heart to tell him it is either that or go insane. I hope that theme is obvious throughout the book. Don't take any of it too seriously, and enjoy the ride. If you can't laugh at yourself, put down the book and walk away slowly... Otherwise, read on with a sense of humor and a bit of cynicism. With the direction this world is headed, man, we are going to need plenty of both!

The ideas I share were born in the trench warfare I call "business," born from making painful mistakes and from getting fired from corporate America because I don't suffer fools very well (and there is this little issue about my problem with authority...).

I have been consulting with business owners for more than twenty years. As I began this book, we were in the middle of a global economic meltdown. The rules changed in the fall of 2008 and most people were not ready. People were riding the credit gravy train thinking the ride would never end. Many lived in houses and drove cars they could not afford. A lot of business owners who lived their personal lives this way also ran their businesses in the same way. Need more money? Tap into the equity of your house! Need a house, use a welfare check as verification of income! We all just got bitch-slapped back into reality – hard.

During the "good times," there is no shortage of feel-good philosophies like "team building." My wife and I owned a business coaching franchise for four years. We bought ourselves out of the agreement a year early due to philosophical differences with the accepted practices of the franchise. I was at ground zero with a lot of these feel-good, quick-fix business strategies that seemed to become the norm. I was once in a meeting with about twenty other business coach/franchise owners. Most of the coaches were not making any money so a coach was brought in from another region to do a workshop to help increase sales. At one point, the facilitator asked everybody to stand up and start skipping around the room chanting: "I AM SOMEBODY!" I was livid. This type of an exercise is complete BS and if you think this will help increase sales and take your business to the next level, try therapy first. This is just one example of kumbaya nonsense, and it is rampant in and out of corporate America.

In down economies, what are some of the first expenses to be cut in corporate America? HR and team-building exercises. Seems rather ironic. If this stuff actually worked, wouldn't the companies need them more than ever? In all of those exercises that I have had the misfortune of sitting through, I have never seen any of them make long-term changes in *anybody's* behavior. My personal belief is that HR exists in corporate America to help companies navigate the crushing number of rules imposed by the government and to try to stop employee lawsuits by making employees think the company actually cares.

The same thing holds true for sales training. I know the president of a company that does sales training worldwide for the big software companies. They each cancelled some or all of their sales training for 2009. So, let me get this straight, sales are down so they *cancel* sales training? Sales are up so they schedule sales training? Something seems backwards here. Why invest in sales training and team-building exercises only in good economies if they really work? Wouldn't the best time to do these exercises be in a down economy, because that is when you would need them the most? I'm just asking...

Another one of the philosophies making the rounds is the "power of attraction." In short we attract success or failure with our thoughts, or some crap like that. With the world economic system in the tank, what happened? Did everybody start thinking negative thoughts at once? Look at Iceland, the poster child of the credit-leveraging binge. Did everyone in Iceland suddenly decide at the same time they did not like their new standard of living and so let's bankrupt the country and go back to fishing? How about Ireland? How about all of the other countries around the world whose economies are in shambles? Time to get real.

Now business owners have to get back to the basics of running a business: Be a good leader, know how to sell, and manage your numbers – no "secrets," no feel-good daily affirmations, just common business sense.

The odds are stacked against you...

There are three kinds of lies: lies, damned lies and statistics.
~ Mark Twain

According to the Small Business Administration Office of Advocacy, two-thirds of new businesses survive at least two years, forty-four percent survive at least four years, and thirty-three percent survive at least seven years[1]

If you knew you were about to sink your 401k (what is left of it) into an investment with a fifty-six percent chance of failing in four years, would you do it? Probably not! Despite these odds, every year more than 600,000 new companies are opened[2]. Most of these budding entrepreneurs are clueless about running a business. They don't like sales, they don't understand a financial statement, and they think leadership is being their employees' friend.

The American dream hype says that anybody can run a successful business. Sorry, not true. The hype also says that being your own boss is your ticket to freedom and fortune. Sorry, again. For most that is not

1 http://www.sba.gov/advo/stats/sbfaq.pdf, July 2009.
2 Ibid.

true, either. More than half the time the dream turns into a nightmare. It does not have to be this way. Armed with the right knowledge, some blind faith, and a little luck, some of us *can* have the American dream. When one succeeds, life is good. When one fails, it can be hell on earth.

This book is based on my experiences in business for more than thirty years, as an employee, executive, business owner, and business coach/consultant. In sharing my experiences and observations I hope to bring a reality check to those who are trying to run a business. I undertook this endeavor to cut through the hype and myths presented in most self-help business books. Sorry, folks, but there is no magic bullet or secret strategy to turning a business around. It takes hard work, luck, and the ability to get out of your own way. J. Paul Getty, at one time the richest man in the world, wrote in *How To Be Rich*: "There are no absolutely safe or sure-fire formulas for achieving success in business." What he wrote in the middle of the last century is still true.

I hope to provide some relief to the stress and self-doubt of business owners who read the how-to books on small business and cannot get the advice offered to work. "You mean all I have to do is create a set of processes and my business will run without me?"

If only it were that easy...

I hope my message can be seen as a breath of fresh air: (Finally! Somebody who feels like I do and is willing to say the emperor has no clothes!) I do try to be uplifting and inspirational, but I also know that the "average" person cannot handle the stress of making payroll with their American Express card or hoping beyond hope that the invoice gets paid on time so they can cover the payroll taxes on Friday. Not everyone is cut out to be a small business owner. Being an entrepreneur takes guts, courage in the face of fire, high tolerance for risk, a strong work ethic, a fierce level of independence, a sense of pride in a job well done, and the self-confidence to keep going after being knocked down. New economic conditions test the mettle of every entrepreneur. The spending spree leading up to the meltdown in 2008 might someday seem like the good ol' days.

So, I am compelled to lampoon some sacred cows and blast some business philosophies that are hawked to unsuspecting business owners as the gospel truth. But I also provide ideas and tips I have found to be successful in my career and with my clients, as well.

I have helped business owners see double-digit increases in revenue and profits using real-world, sometimes in-your-face, street-smart strategies – not strategies based on tapping into quantum psychics or magic bullets. These entrepreneurs succeeded by accepting outside counsel, having a willingness to look at new ideas, and executing what they learned. Although I provide ideas and suggestions for taking a business to the next level, I do not recommend that all of my suggestions and strategies be followed. Frankly, they shouldn't be. What works for some will not work for others. No book can do the hard work for you – you have to do it yourself!

SECTION I

ENTREPRENEURSHIP

CHAPTER 1

CONFESSIONS OF A BUSINESS COACH...

The day after tomorrow is the third day of the rest of your life.
~ George Carlin

I was at dinner with a group of business owners and we were discussing the pending publication of this book. One of the owners said he was very interested in my book because, "I don't read business books very often, but when I do, I just assume they must be right..." Truer words have never been spoken. So many people read a business book and just assume it must be right because it is in print. There is a lot of garbage out there disguised as business advice. We are led to believe that if we just follow a simple set of step-by-step instructions, anybody can build a successful business. If that were the case, why aren't all businesses successful? And using that logic, doesn't it make sense that anybody with a step-by-step business book would be a successful business coach or consultant? After all, they have an instruction book.

There are a lot of very good business coaches/consultants, both in and out of franchise organizations. But unfortunately, they are in the minority. The dirty little secret in the business coaching/consulting world is that most business coaches/consultants are struggling to make a living. The lucky ones have a spouse who is bringing in some income. How can that be if they have the instruction manual for success? How do you coach another business to success if you can't make money in your own business? You can't.

As I mentioned, my wife and I owned a business coaching franchise for four years so let me just get this out of the way: business coaching works, sometimes. There is a very important caveat – you have to find the right coach for you and your business. If not, it is a waste of time and money. In my first year, I was the North American Rookie of the Year and the Georgia Coach of the Year for the franchise. I was a successful coach in the system, but was I the most successful coach? Nope. Could I have been? Probably. But frankly I just did not want to work the hours those coaches did. I also stopped "drinking the Kool-Aid."

For the majority of my clients, my coaching was very successful. For others it did not work. Why some and not others? Why not all? It would be easy to tell you the reasons my clients were successful. It's much harder to look at why the coaching did not work. But that is when we learn – when we fail. So when I lose a client, I try and take an honest look at what happened. I found that there are many reasons for the coaching process to fail and there is plenty of blame to spread around. Some examples: My personality did not fit with my client; I failed to deliver to the client's expectations; the client waited too long to ask for help and could (or would) not get out of the ditch; or the client frankly should not have been in business in the first place. But the number-one reason I have found for failure is the inability for business owners to get out of their own way. This fatal leadership flaw has crashed many a business.

As a coach you sometimes have to be tough with your clients to help them break through whatever obstacles are in their way. If the coach is too worried about losing a client because of their own personal cash-flow situation, the coach will be hesitant to rock the boat. I know; I have been there.

I know of another coaching company that uses employees to do the coaching. Does an employee really know what it is like to be a business owner? No. And I don't care how much training they have had, or what handbook they follow, employees and owners live in two different worlds.

Ultimately, it boils down to the experiences and knowledge of the coach and how applicable they are to the client's circumstances. Some coaches are more "life" coaches than "business" coaches. Which is fine if that is what you signed up for. Their sessions tend to be more like therapy sessions than about business practices. But the reality is that most businesses who hire a coach don't have time for therapy sessions. They need results and they need them now. Often, the "business" part of this type of coaching is: "Here, read this book; everybody is reading it... Now let's do an exercise where we think positive thoughts and imagine our sales increasing." Like I said, that is fine if that is what you signed up for, but just don't expect your sales to increase.

Unfortunately, too many coaches use the latest hyped book as a base for their coaching sessions because they do not have a business foundation upon which to help business owners. Bottom line: make sure you find the right coach for you and your business. If you do, that person really can help you turn your business around or take it to the next level. Choose the wrong one and no matter how much you sit around and imagine unicorns and rainbows, your business is not going to change.

CHAPTER 2

THE OTHER SIDE OF "SUCCESS"...

I see dead people.
~ Eight-year-old Cole Sear in *The Sixth Sense*

I just finished reading an article about an entrepreneur who turned his last twelve cents into a seventeen-million-dollar company. I have read countless stories like this one – the entrepreneur reaches the heights of success after hitting rock bottom. He slept at work or in his car because he could not afford his own place. He ate peanut butter and showered in the park… And because of his laser-like focus and dedication, he rose from the ashes to reach the heights of success. How many of us have asked the question after reading one of these stories: "What does he have that I don't? I am probably just as smart as he is…"

For every one of these individuals who can focus like a laser on a long-term goal and achieve it, there are countless others who wrote down goals, were just as smart, just as confident, and yet failed to achieve these lofty heights. Why some, but not others? I have a friend who was at one time very successful in one of the largest multi-level network marketing companies in the world (we have all heard of the company). I asked him what the typical success rate was of people in his organization. He estimated one in a hundred. Why? Everybody has the same access to the same literature, seminars, and products. Why some and not others?

So what are some of the common traits of the business owners in these types of "inspirational" stories? (I put the sarcastic quotes around inspirational because I believe most people wind up a bit depressed after reading those articles). For one, there never seem to be any children in the picture. Having never lived in my car, I would assume that it is a lot easier to do when you don't have the responsibility of a family. I saw a *Dr. Phil* show where a father was being accused by his wife's family of child abuse. The family's living conditions were just a step above living in a car because the family was constantly broke due to a continuous series of bad business decisions by the father. The father's perspective was that he had some business dreams that had not yet come to fruition and success was just around the corner. Everybody just needed to wait a little longer. I could not help thinking what would have been the outcome of the "twelve cent" story if there had been children involved. In addition, you rarely hear about a spouse in such stories and, when you do, it usually involves a divorce.

Is this an excuse? Hell, no – just one of the realities of life. So what happens to the single-minded drive of the entrepreneur when there is a family involved? The drive usually gets sidelined. You can't have both, so stop believing the hype. I know of a man who owns numerous successful businesses. In his speaking engagements he likes to say he took a couple of years off to be with his children and had somebody else run his businesses. He had a president to run his company, but he still kept calling all the shots. His kids? They each had their own nanny. Reality does not match the hype.

Very little is written about the FULL price of a single-minded quest. The price rarely mentioned can be measured in failed relationships, financial ruin, or deteriorating health. Usually a nasty mixture of all three.

Most of us struggle to find the right balance between business and family. It is my opinion that you can't have it all. For those rare individuals who *seem* to have it all, congratulations. But they are probably not reading this book anyway. I would venture to guess if we had a chance to *really* look behind the curtain, we would see that they have the same boatloads of problems we all have – they just have a nicer place to play with their dysfunctions.

When I was growing up in the seventies, women were first told (and continue to be told) that they can have it all. A woman could be a wife, a mother, and have a full-time career. What a crock. Something has to give and it looks like it is our sanity and our health.

According to a 2005 study by the U.S. Centers for Disease Control and Prevention, 2.4 billion drugs were prescribed in visits to doctors and hospitals in 2005[1]. Of those, 118 million were for antidepressants. According to the CDC, antidepressants are the most-prescribed drugs in the U.S. and adult use of antidepressants almost tripled between the periods 1988-1994 and 1999-2000. High blood pressure drugs were the next most common with 113 million prescriptions. Studies have shown that most heart attacks occur on Monday mornings between the hours of nine and eleven. Connected? I think so. The quest for the bigger car, bigger house, bigger watch, better body, has a price. And it is very expensive, and it is not just money. Now, you can't say you weren't warned…

---

1 http://www.cnn.com/2007/HEALTH/07/09/antidepressants/index.html, May 2009.

CHAPTER 3

JUST BECAUSE YOU ARE IN BUSINESS DOES NOT MEAN YOU SHOULD BE...

You want answers?
I want the truth!
You can't handle the truth!
~ Col. Nathan R. Jessop in *A Few Good Men*, 1992

In my experience working with hundreds of small businesses, I found that most business owners should really find another occupation. Most will not seek outside counsel, much less read a book. I have seen business owners "rearranging the deck chairs on the Titanic" because they were convinced that their way is right. They feel like if they just work a little harder (as if eighty-plus hours a week is not enough), they can turn it around. When that does not work, they get the bright idea that going deeper into debt is the answer. "Throw more money at it! That will fix it!" Huh? Just because the government does it, does not mean it is a viable solution. Even as the ship is disappearing under the waves, these folks still look everywhere else for the reasons for their failure. The human ego is a powerful entity.

A canary in a coal mine is a metaphor for an early warning of danger or trouble yet to come. In the nineteenth and twentieth centuries, miners brought canaries into the mines with them as an early warning device to detect the build-up of gases such as methane and carbon monoxide. The theory was that canaries could detect these gases much sooner than the miners. If the canaries stopped singing, became agitated, or died, the miners knew immediately to evacuate the mine shaft because lethal levels of gas were building up. In the "mine" of small business, the canary is on life support. No matter which statistics you care to believe, the great majority of small businesses never see their fifth-year anniversary. In fact, most never make a profit. In other words, the majority of the miners are not going to make it out of the mine.

Something is very wrong with this picture. Why? What are some of the main reasons businesses fail? First, start with the owner: ego, pride, ignorance and, sometimes, just plain stupidity can conspire to take down a business. Second: lack of cash. Third: the employees. They are your greatest asset and biggest liability. Take to the playing field with the wrong team and you are toast. Now combine these with the plethora of bad or misleading information guiding business owners in the wrong direction and you can see why so many fail.

Now just for fun, add rising costs, stifling tax laws, burdensome government regulations, and intense competition. No wonder business owners have it hard. The result is legions of struggling and broke business owners searching for the Holy Grail of business knowledge that will lead their business into the Promised Land.

Out of their desperation comes a huge industry built around helping business owners succeed. From "snake oil" salesmen pushing "everything you need to know to make your business succeed," to New Age philosophies disguised as business strategies, the business owner is inundated with "get rich quick" schemes. I have yet to find a book that, if followed step by step, would lead to a successful company.

After working with hundreds of small businesses and a corporate career in sales, I have reached the following conclusions:

- It is disingenuous and a fraud to suggest that everybody can succeed in business. We are bombarded with books and seminars proclaiming that EVERYBODY can get rich if they just follow the latest ten steps to success. It is just not true and it breaks my heart every time I meet business owners about to lose their home and everything they own because they were under the delusion they could run a business.

- Despite what the politically correct crowd wants us to believe, this is a dog-eat-dog world where the strongest, smartest, and prettiest have the greatest chances to succeed. We are not all created equal. Some people are smarter, some are better athletes, and some are better looking. Just a fact of life – get used to it. If life were fair and we were all created equal, how come I am not making gazillions of dollars playing in the NFL?

- The majority of business owners will never be rich. In fact, they will be lucky to break even. If you don't agree with me, take another look at the statistics of business failure.
- Those that have succeeded have the skill sets (most innate and some learned) to prosper no matter what "strategy" du jour is in front of them. Sometimes it is luck, other times brute force of will, and other times it is just sheer tenacity to get the job done.

Yes, there are always the rags-to-riches stories. One of the best examples is the movie *The Pursuit of Happyness* with Will Smith, which is based on an extraordinary individual named Chris Gardner. Mr. Gardner is not just an average person who, despite incredible odds and with unbelievable tenacity, turned his life around. There is something in his DNA that would not let him quit, and that is something that cannot be taught. The average person would have quit in the first thirty minutes of the movie. It is the same in business as in life. Circumstances can take seemingly average people and turn them into extraordinary individuals, but there has to be something in their DNA to work with in the first place.

There are plenty of motivational speakers out there who will say that everybody has it in them to be extraordinary. I guess that life has made me too cynical to share that sentiment. My experience has shown that most people do not want to be extraordinary and will go out of their way to prove it. Just ask any person who has to manage a staff. As the saying goes: You can't fix stupid…

Having interviewed and worked with hundreds of small companies in all business sectors, I have found that there are many reasons businesses fail or succeed. At the top of the list is the number-one asset and liability of every small business: the owner. Here are five traits of a business owner that can kill a business.

- They do not like change.
- They are poor leaders.
- They do not understand the financial aspects of their business.

- They do not like "sales."
- They hire the wrong employees (and then can't fire them).

Some can be fixed; others cannot. For example, hiring the wrong employees can be fixed. As far as becoming a better leader is concerned, I am not so sure this can be taught. I have rarely seen unnatural leaders transform themselves into highly effective models of leadership. In fact, I can't remember *any*, now that I think about it...

CHAPTER 4

THE RULES ALWAYS CHANGE...

There are three rules to running a business; fortunately, we don't know any of them.
~ Paul Newman

The set of financial rules that most of us went by for so long changed in 2008. And they continue to change, and change quickly. We entered a global recession; our investments took a beating, and the massive government debt continued to grow to the point most people cannot even comprehend. The government just threw out trillions of dollars of the taxpayer's money at the problem like it was a trip to the mall.

You may be one of those who were living on the "credit gravy train." You know, living on the equity in your house and sitting on huge credit card debt to finance that "living large" lifestyle. If so, the time came to pay the piper.

A friend of mine called to tell me about an acquaintance who was moving his family into his in-laws' house. About six months earlier, he had been downsized from a $200,000-plus annual income selling software. He had a very nice house and a wife who stayed home with the three kids. He felt like he had done everything right, gave to the church, put money in his 401k and had a six- to eight-month reserve for such an emergency. Then the "perfect storm" hit – he lost his job; the job market shrank significantly, and his portfolio took a beating. He no longer had a six- to eight-month reserve. His story did not make complete sense so I asked my friend a few questions. Turns out he was sitting on almost forty thousand in credit card debt. Oh yeah, they just put sixty thousand into a new kitchen at the beginning of the year. How many cars? At least three. Yet this guy felt he had done everything right. Why? Because everybody he knew was doing the same thing. The rules changed for him – quickly and harshly.

If you ran a business the same way, chances are you would be circling the drain unless you made some drastic and immediate changes. I have seen so many business owners who think cash flow is the same as profits. They keep accepting unprofitable business in order to keep paying the bills and then putting the difference on credit. All the while assuming, "I will make it up next month." One day they look up and notice they are deep in debt with no real hope of getting out. Sadly, a lot of them are surprised when they find out just how deep a hole they have dug for themselves. Our ability as humans to delude ourselves never ceases to amaze me.

Those who chose not to ride the "credit gravy train" landed in a position of strength compared to their competitors. They were able to use their advantage to strike and strike hard at their competitors to gain market share. Those who struggled even during the good times had to buckle up for a bumpy ride! For the aggressive and willing, there is always an abundance of opportunity amidst this type of chaos and confusion.

Every serious businessperson better be looking at *everything* differently and not get too comfortable…

CHAPTER 5

THERE IS NO MAGIC FORMULA FOR SUCCESS...

There are no absolutely safe or sure-fire formulas for achieving success in business.
~ J. Paul Getty, *How To Be Rich*

I have met countless business owners who are very smart and ambitious, yet their business struggles or fails. I have also met people who can't seem to get out of their own way when running their business, but they are still successful. Why? There is no canned answer for this unfair reality of life. It is just a mix of skill and luck. The individual *and* the process, and being at the right place at the right time.

According to many of the self-help business books, just follow the system and your business will succeed. Unfortunately, it doesn't work that way. The problem is that strategies that worked for one business owner will not necessarily work for another. There is not a magic formula or a canned process for success. If this were not the case, then why is it when groups of business owners (i.e. franchise) are given the same tools, only a small percentage actually succeed?

There are tens of thousands of how-to books for small business to choose from. In the fall of 2008, I did a search for "small business" on Amazon.com. The search returned 105,483 books (the fact that you are reading this book tells me I beat the odds in some small way. Thank you!). On Amazon, I can buy a used copy of a book for $7.15 and get: "Everything I need to know to succeed in my small business." And for just ten dollars, I can get: "Everything I need to know to start up and run my business."

If only it were that easy…

I have a theory why most of these books do not work as advertised, especially if you are using them as a how-to or step-by-step training manual; WE ARE NOT ALL THE SAME. Personality, attitude, work ethic, religious beliefs, knowledge of business, baggage from childhood, self-perception, and education all have a direct impact on the success or failure of a business.

Now let's add the products you sell, the price of your products, the gross profit on each product, your customers, your employees (if there are any), overhead required to sell and deliver the products, and the area of the country or world where you and your customers live. One size fits all? It is impossible. No two businesses are the same. Eighty percent of the mechanics of a business are the same (A/R, A/P, etc.), but the personalities and details never are. These variables will make or break a business. With this many variables, is it any wonder that step-by-step books do not typically work?

There are too many people and books promoting a false hope and it pisses me off. I have seen numerous people start doubting themselves after reading one of these books because they cannot make it work like in the book. "Real life" does not have a step-by-step manual, neither does business.

After reading way too many of these books and even recommending them to my clients, I started noticing some very interesting things. Most business owners do not read. The number-one excuse is that they don't have time.

Some of these books are what I describe as "getting drunk on the Kool-Aid" books. They go something like this: Follow these three life-changing philosophies and you can have anything you ever imagined! Just send $29.95 and you can have the secrets that unlock the wealth of universe!

Some of these books are too theoretical for small business. Running a Fortune 500 company is very different than running a small business.

Conclusion? These books rarely change behavior in the long run.

The number-one problem with most businesses is the owner – not the product, the competition, or the economy. To change your business, you have to start with yourself.

CHAPTER 6

IGNORANCE IS NOT BLISS – IT IS EXPENSIVE...

*The recipe for perpetual ignorance is: Be satisfied with your opinions
and content with your knowledge.*
~ Elbert Hubbard

It is amazing how many people don't "have time" to read. Reading is
one of the few things that can change our perspective and expand our
vision. However, my advice to people reading this, or any other advice
book, is to read all of it with a grain of salt. Some advice works, some
doesn't. Some ideas work for some people, but not for others. But in order
to find what works for you, read, read, read.

The majority of self-help business books are just a rehash of *Think
and Grow Rich* by Napoleon Hill. If you are not inclined to read, just buy
these three books and you will get the gist of the rest of the books.

1. *Think and Grow Rich*, Napoleon Hill
2. *How To Be Rich*, J. Paul Getty
3. *The Greatest Salesman in the World*, Og Mandino

You might notice a slight paradox in my sentiments about business
books. Why read them if they don't work? They do work – but not in
the way most people expect. I find that, for me, reading is like putting
together a puzzle. At points, sometimes totally unexpectedly, something
I read comes back like a piece of a puzzle I am trying to solve and the
solution(s) fall into place. Sun Tzu's *The Art of War* did that for me. Other
books make me realize that there is a whole other part of the puzzle I
did not know existed. *The Black Swan* by Nassim Nicholas Taleb was like

that for me. In fact, I told a colleague that I was not sure if I was getting smarter or really screwing myself up reading that book. The jury is still out on that one...

Bottom line: the more I read, the more I realize how ignorant I really am.

CHAPTER 7

GOING TO A SEMINAR AND BUYING A BUNCH OF BOOKS IS NOT GOING TO FIX YOUR BUSINESS...

Thank you, sir! Can I have another?
~ Chip Diller in *Animal House*

Running a business is hard. Real hard. Because of that, there is a huge industry (i.e. this book) built around helping people succeed. Unfortunately, there is a lot of Kool-Aid drinking and "group think" that occurs by people desperately seeking answers. Part of the business self-help industry preys on this desire by providing false hopes and trying to make you feel stupid if you are not enlightened enough to get their message.

I have given and attended countless seminars and I have discovered something that seems like common sense: Going to a seminar and buying a bunch of books will not fix a business. There are seminar junkies that keep going in search of the magic bullet that will get them out of the situation they are currently in. I attended a seminar where every five minutes or so, we were supposed to turn to the person next to us and give a high five and tell each other that we are great. Yeah, that really works... The purpose of a lot of these seminars seems more to be designed to make you to feel good and buy their stuff.

I was at a seminar where they "packaged" ten books by the speaker. At the break they announced that "for just a few minutes, you can buy all of these books for the low price of..." People lined up to buy them. The majority of those people will never read more than one of those books, let alone all ten. Quoting a friend of mine: "You leave drunk on the Kool-Aid and a couple of days later you find you have a hole in the bottom of your cup."

On another occasion, I attended a "motivational" seminar that included the likes of Rudy Giuliani and Jimmy Carter. One of the speakers was regaling everybody about how easy it was to get rich in the stock market – you just had to use the totally amazing, incredible software that tells you when to buy and sell. He even gave us a brief demonstration. After he thoroughly whet everyone's appetite and had the audience believing they all could be millionaires by this time next month, he announced that for the first fifty or one hundred people (I don't remember the exact number), and for today only, you could attend the first class for only $99.00 (credit cards only). Money back guarantee! Pointing to the tables behind the stage, he let us know that "associates were ready to take your registration" but for only a limited time and for a limited number of people. Before he could even finish his sentence, people were literally running to the tables to sign up with their credit cards flashing. Do you think more than the original "limited number" of people signed up? Absolutely. Pathetic example of group think. Brilliant marketing.

At my son's swim meet, I saw a fellow bored parent reading *How to Implement G.E.'s Revolutionary Method for Busting Bureaucracy.* I laughed out loud. The fact that anybody believes that G.E. does not have bureaucracy and can get a two-inch thick book printed is a perfect example of drinking the Kool-Aid. Just put G.E. in the title and it must be right! Just take a look at their stock price... Oh, *never mind.*

There are numerous books about and from Jack Welch (ex-president of General Electric). If you believe the press, Jack is the end-all in leadership examples—the icon we all strive to be. I came across another book, *At Any Cost,* that takes direct aim at Jack Welch and G.E., even to the point of saying Jack's management style affected national divorce rates. Wow, which book to believe?

There is another business philosophy that is characterized by the term, "Create a vacuum..." and it really bugs me. You will see it in some of the more metaphysically based business philosophies. According to this philosophy, nature abhors a vacuum. So if you buy that expensive car, or lease new office space, or any expenditure you can't really afford right now, "nature" will fill the vacuum in your cash flow created by your new purchase. Somehow "nature" will start magically bringing you the new customers (and money) to fill the vacuum. I have seen many business owners go broke waiting for the vacuum to be filled. When we are in a global recession, how does that work again?

Beware of these feel-good, group-think activities. They are everywhere and they are disguised as books, seminars, and workshops. In order for your business to succeed, you do have to have a goal and the faith that you are going to reach it. But you also have to execute – just "thinking about it" or writing it down is not enough.

During my career, I have begun to notice something very interesting about the human condition – we have this innate need to put everything in a neat little box to try and make sense of it. When the market forces are up and times are good, people can be successful in spite of themselves. Because we have the need to put everything into a box, we look for the reasons we are successful. From this need sprouts business strategies wrapped up in New Age philosophies or other such nonsense. Few want to admit it can't be because the blind squirrel can get lucky and find an acorn every now and then; it has to be because I have tapped into prosperity at the quantum physics level of the universe. Right? Besides, this sounds a lot cooler than I just got lucky...

CHAPTER 8

You will always work "in" your business...

A businessman must run his own business. He cannot expect his employees to think or do as well as he can. If they could, they would not be his employees.
~ J. Paul Getty, *How To Be Rich*, 1961

One of the more popular small business philosophies is: "Work on your business, not in it." Another is: "Build a business that works without you." I have worked with countless business owners who have been introduced to one or both of these philosophies and have become very frustrated. Why? It seems so easy in the book! I feel the need to clarify these because I found there is a lot of confusion and frustration surrounding these ideas.

On paper it looks so easy. The problem is that most small business owners are too busy doing the day-to-day tactical stuff to actually "work on" the business. I don't know how many times I have heard a frustrated business owner say, "I don't have time to do all I have to do now; when am I going to find time to work on my business!" The problem is they are usually under-capitalized so they can't afford to hire a general manager to run their business while they are "working on it." Or they are control freaks and don't know how to delegate.

The frustrations stem from the chaos of running a business and the corresponding lack of time to do everything. I was speaking with an owner of a hair salon who had just finished one of these books and was kicking herself because she could not figure out how to do it all. She desperately wanted to "get out from behind the chair," but she was one of the biggest moneymakers. If she stopped working "in" the business, there would be no business to work "on." She felt it must be that she was doing something wrong because the book made it look so easy. The simple truth is that until you have the capital to hire a general manager to run your business, you are going to be working full-time "in" it.

Most people mistakenly think that working on the business means having a business that works without you. It does not. If you want your business to succeed, you will always be working in it and on it. You may not be turning the screwdriver, but you are in it. The general premise is that if you build all of the right processes and hire the right people, the business will run itself. I disagree. Have you seen this story?

A budding entrepreneur borrows $50,000 from his parents to start a business. He starts by building the processes. He then hires a staff to run the processes. Voila! He now has a successful business that works without him and off he runs to live on a boat!

I haven't ever seen this happen. If you could so easily create one of these businesses, everybody would have a successful business.

We have all read a magazine story about the person living on their boat making a six-figure income (notice, no kids…). Assuming they are not running drugs, how many of these people have a business that works without them? They may be living on a boat but, odds are, they are still working their asses off. Unless you are an investor, I personally think that for most business owners, having a business that works without you is a pipedream.

Look at Jack Welch and G.E. – arguably one of THE business success stories, top of the heap. Under Jack Welch, G.E. turned out more CEOs and executives for other companies than probably any other business in history. Under Jack, G.E. constantly cut the bottom ten percent of employees in a continual plan of upgrading employees. So it is safe to say that Jack was surrounded by the best supporting staff in business. Did Jack have a business that ran without him? Absolutely not! Jack lived on a G.E. corporate jet and worked seven days a week. Why did he have to work seven days a week if he had the best employees? Because it takes leaders to run a business. The leader is working *on* the business, and he is working *in* the business.

As your business grows, you trade one set of problems for another.

For example, you will find as your business grows, some of your employees can no longer cut it. They have a skill set that worked well for a smaller business, but no longer. The problems never go away; they just come at you faster as the business grows. You will always struggle with employees, managing cash and staying in front of the competition. Can you leave your business in the hands of an employee? Sure. But for how long? What happens if they leave? If they are that good, are they going to be satisfied watching you live on the boat while they do all the work? No, I don't think so. Moral of the story is that for the majority of small business owners, it will be years before you can spend the majority of your time working "on" the business, but you will *always* be "in" it.

CHAPTER 9

IT IS NEVER GOING TO BE PERFECT...

We have a "strategic" plan. It's called doing things.
~ Herb Kelleher, founder, Southwest Airlines

We hear so much about having goals and plans; we assume that we are probably the only ones without them. The truth is, almost every business owner I have met does not have them, either. Most people run their business day to day, looking two feet in front of them. Long-term planning is making the next payroll.

Can you predict the future? To some extent you can in the short term. For example, "If I do not get paid on that invoice by Thursday, I cannot pay my payroll taxes on Monday, and now I owe interest and penalties." You do have an impact on the future by decisions you make, both good and bad.

Can you forecast next month's sales? Yes, if you have a good sales process in place. How about next years? Or three years out? Five? Not really. The longer the time frame of the forecast, it exponentially reduces in accuracy. However, that does not mean you do not set a target to shoot at. I personally believe that for most small business owners a ninety-day sales forecast is wishful thinking. Too many things can happen in three months to affect the forecast – most of which are out of your control and most of which are not good. That does not mean you do not have a ninety-day forecast. What it means is that you shoot for a number and be prepared to make changes to how you are going to get that number.

So what happens when something comes out of left field that completely changes your forecasts and goals? For example: You have been told that your company is going to be awarded the big contract in the next quarter. Your contact at the company says it is a "done deal," just needs one more meeting – just a formality. Next thing you know, the company goes through a downsizing. Your contact is let go and your project is cancelled. Did you plan for that?

How about 9/11? Did that have an impact on your business? Nassim Nicholas Taleb describes this type of an event as a "black swan" in his book *The Black Swan – The Impact of the Highly Improbable*. A black swan is an event that you cannot predict happening that substantially changes the status quo. Are you prepared for the next black swan? Are you factoring into next year's budget another natural disaster on the scale of Hurricane Katrina? Or a low-yield nuclear device being detonated in a U.S. city?

My personal belief is that creating a three- to five-year plan with financial budgets for a small business is just a waste of time. Business moves too quickly and there will be another black swan in the next two or three years, maybe sooner. Did you plan for the market meltdown of September 2008? Oops, another black swan...

How about marketing plans? They do not need to be longer than a few pages. Any longer and it just sits on the shelf.

Please understand that I am not saying that having goals and plans is a bad idea. In fact you should have both. I have each of my clients prepare a budget for the next twelve months. The primary reason is to take a look at cash flow. It is not meant to be a budget that is rigorously followed but as a guideline. I know – there is some anal-retentive control freak having a meltdown right now about how wrong I am. I have found that most people are just not that disciplined and they are not going to follow it religiously anyway; so why kid ourselves? Another reason is that in a twelve-month period, it is going to change several times due to events that are both in and out of our control. Nature has a way of messing with us that way.

My wife was a member of a professional businesswomen's group. Every month they had a guest speaker. One particular meeting the presenter was a financial planner. To back up her point, she cited a Harvard Study of Goal Setting that most of us have heard of if we have been to more than one seminar. The story goes something like this:

> *A group of researchers asked a class at Harvard how many had written goals. The study found that three percent had written down their goals, ten percent had goals in their head but not written, and the rest did not have a clue. Years later the class was surveyed and they found that the three percent who had written down their goals made ten times the income than those who did not write down their goals.*

I took the time (all fifteen minutes) to research this study, and read that it was conducted in the 1950s. Another source said it was conducted at Yale. According to one famous business book, the date was 1979. One story said thirteen percent of the class who had goals was earning, on average, twice as much as the eighty-four percent who had no goals at all. So what was it? Yale or Harvard? 1950 or 1979? Twice as much or ten times as much?

The magazine *Fast Company* actually did some real research and found that this story is unfortunately an urban myth[1]. They even went to the titans of personal achievement and motivational speakers, Anthony Robbins, Brian Tracy, and Zig Ziglar to get their source for the story. Oops, seems records were destroyed or they pointed to each other as the source.

Ouch, Anthony Robbins, Brian Tracy, and Zig Ziglar... the big guys... Guess I won't be getting them to endorse this book...

---

1 http://www.fastcompany.com/magazine/06/cdu.html, December 8, 2007.

CHAPTER 10

THERE IS NEVER ENOUGH TIME TO DO IT ALL...

I am definitely going to take a course in time management…
just as soon as I can work it into my schedule.
~ Louis E. Boone

A common trait I find amongst business owners is their belief that they have to do everything because they can do it better. This is probably true. Get used to it and move on. I had one business owner tell me that if he can find somebody who can do the task "seventy-five percent as good" as he can, he will hire that person. Chances are that the employee can do the tasks much better than "seventy-five percent as good" as the owner. But we know most business owners have healthy egos so we will just leave it at that…

This brings up another very important concept – delegation. I am a great delegator. I once had an employee tell me: "Man, you delegate everything!" Why am I a great delegator? I like to work smarter not harder. Delegation also means giving your employees the latitude to complete the task their way. As long as they can complete the task in the time allotted and the outcome is what was expected – who cares how they did it? I get clients all the time who are frustrated because their employees will not do the tasks exactly as they do. I have had the following conversation numerous times:

Me: "Why does it matter how they do it?"
Business owner: "Because my way is better!"
Me: "Better than what? Is the outcome the same?"

Business owner: "Yes, but…"

Me: "But what?"

Business owner: "Oh, shut up…"

Time management is the bane of every entrepreneur. Never enough time and always too much to do. Funny thing about time, it is the one thing we really have control over. But it is also the one thing most of us feel we never have enough of. Delegation helps with time management. But the problem is not time, it is usually prioritizing the tasks we have in conjunction with the available time.

There is a huge market for time management tools: day planners, PDAs, websites, books, just to name a few. How many of us have had one or all of these, usually in multiples? The truth is: most of us. I was just reading a book about creating a sales machine. One of the first things it espouses is time management. The author has a comprehensive system for managing your time and the employee's time. While reading this book, I had an epiphany. These systems were designed by anal-retentive control freaks. They probably work very well for other anal-retentive control freaks, but not for me, and maybe not for you, either.

I can't remember the number of these systems I have looked at, and/or tried, and I always seem to go back to a mix of a tablet of paper and Outlook. Look at the pretty day planner that manages everything, including my goals and when I go to the bathroom… Why won't it work for me? Plain and simple, because I don't think that way.

I keep to-do lists because, at my age, remembering where I put my car keys can be an exercise in futility. The problem with most people's lists is that there is too much on them. Most of which they will never get to anyway, because there are not enough hours in a day. An over-packed to-do list is like a death of a thousand cuts, but all self-inflicted. How many times have you put some incredibly important task (that had to be done today or the world ends) on your to-do list and then discovered a week later that you never got around to doing it? Way too many to count… and guess what? The world did not end; did it? I had a client freaking out over an item on his to-do list that was more than four years old! Yes, he was an anal-retentive control freak.

CHAPTER 11

ATTENTION ALL REFUGEES FROM CORPORATE AMERICA!

*Human beings were not meant to sit in little cubicles, staring at computer screens
all day, filling out useless forms and listening to eight different bosses
drone on about mission statements.*
~ Peter Gibbons in *Office Space*

I want to sound an early warning siren for prospective first-time business owners. Unfortunately, given all of the corporate layoffs and the difficulty in finding a new job, starting a new business may be the only option for some. Prior to September 2008, most people used their investments or 401Ks to fund their start-ups. Once most of us saw our 401Ks battered, we had even less money to start a business. We must go into this new venture with eyes wide open because the security net is a lot smaller.

Sheryl Crow sang about having "never been there but the brochure looks nice." Owning a business and being my own boss is something I would never trade. As I write this, I cannot imagine *ever* working for somebody else again – EVER. Having said that, the brochure for owning a small business and reality NEVER matches. As I have said before, running a business is NOT for everybody.

Owning and running a small business has very little resemblance to the world of a boss and a paycheck. You work harder and probably make much less money. You have to pay for your own health care and all of your payroll taxes. And oh yeah, nobody is matching your 401K anymore...

Some may say, "But I will buy a franchise. That will be different!"

In response, I offer this challenge. The next time you are in a franchised business, see if you can spot the owner. That person will probably be behind the cash register filling in for the sixteen-year-old employee who did not show up. They are the ones trying to manage hourly workers who really don't give a damn, while silently screaming: "Where is HR? What happened to my six-figure income? Nobody said *I* had to clean the bathroom!" In general they are the ones with the shell-shocked look. Owning a business rarely looks like the brochure…

So why do it? I do it for the freedom—freedom to make my own decisions, make my own rules and control my own destiny. If freedom is not that important to you – then get a regular job and save yourself lots of money and heartache.

CHAPTER 12

OKAY, MR. CYNICAL SMARTY PANTS… NOW WHAT DO I DO?

That's it! You people have stood in my way long enough. I'm going to clown college!
~ Homer Simpson

Remember that there is no magic bullet for success or for fixing your business.

Look in the mirror and do an honest assessment. Be very honest with yourself as to whether you are cut out to own and run a business. In the same way that having a corporate job is not for me, being an entrepreneur may not be right for you. Neither one of us is right or wrong, so just be honest. Take a behavioral assessment to help determine if you are wired to be an entrepreneur. You can't fake being an entrepreneur. If you try to fake it, you will just go broke.

Educate yourself and change your perspective.

Read, read, and then read some more. Reading is the very best way to expand your knowledge and change your perspective. The other day I had a client ask me, "How did you get so smart?" My answer was that I am no smarter than she is; I just read more. I then went home and split an atom in my basement just to see if I could do it. Man, are the neighbors pissed…

Learn to embrace Change.

The ONLY constant in this world is Change. In the 21st century, change is happening at a quicker pace than any time in history. The problem is most people do not like change. Remember: change or go broke.

Keep your goals and plans simple.

Stop trying to make your plans perfect. That is impossible, so stop waiting for all the lights to turn green before leaving your driveway. Make your goals and plans complicated and you just will not do them anyway. Here are some examples of simple goal questions:

- How much money do I want to make?
- How much money do I NEED to make?
- How big do I want my business? (Revenue? Locations? Employees?)
- Do I want a lot of employees? (After this book, probably not...)
- Am I willing to assume a lot of debt in order to reach my goals?
- What is the end game? Sell the business or pass down to the family?

Another method is ask to yourself: What are the top three most important issues facing my company? Let's say the answers are cash flow, leads, and revenue. Now you can build your to-do list around these issues. And every day when you start going down some gopher-hole administrative project, ask yourself, Is this task going to increase my cash flow, generate more leads, or increase sales? Most of the time the answer is going to be, "No," but you do it anyway because it is easier than picking up the phone and calling a prospect.

If you can't figure out what to focus on, here are the top two: sales and cash flow. In the end, nothing else really matters; without them, there is nothing to manage anyway.

Keep your to-do list short and sweet.

Most people cannot effectively handle more than six projects at a time. When we look at a to-do list that has more than six items (and it keeps growing), it only serves to put more stress on an already overloaded system (you).

The problem with most people's to-do lists is not the number of items, but the priority of those items. By keeping it to six, you will be forced to place priorities on the tasks. An easy way to do this is to have short-term (due now) priorities and long-term (due in the future) priorities. For example, you can have four short-term and two long-term items on your to-do list at a time. Priorities will change, so you may need to move items out of the to-do list back into the in-box before they are completed. But keep the to-do list to six items. Right now you may be screaming, "But I have way more than that! I can't do just six!" If you are honest, you will admit that you don't get to most of the items on your to-do list anyway, so just chill out.

The absolute-best method for task management is to delegate as much as possible. If you cannot trust your staff to do some of these tasks, you have to ask yourself the following questions: "Do I have the right employees?" and "Am I a control freak and I can't delegate?" If you have a good staff, then the problem is staring at you in the mirror. If you do not have the right staff, fire them and upgrade the personnel.

Here is my "keep it simple stupid" task-management system:

- Have a to-do list and an in-box.
- Learn to set priorities.
- Keep no more than six items on your active to-do list; all the rest of the tasks go into the in-box.
- When you complete a task on your to-do list, move one from your in-box to the to-do list.
- Delegate, delegate, delegate!

Try this method; it might save your sanity. Oh, by the way… a tablet of paper will do fine.

Stop drinking the Kool-Aid and get real.

Running a successful business is hard work. It takes luck, brains, guts, denial, and a huge set of cojones. Crashing a business can take just as much hard work as building a successful one. Check your ego and bring somebody in from the outside to give you an objective opinion as to what is really going on in your business. An outside perspective could be the best investment in your business you ever make. And it just might save you from going broke…

SECTION II

LEADERSHIP

CHAPTER 13

GET OUT OF YOUR OWN WAY...

A man has got to know his limitations.
~ Harry Callahan in *Dirty Harry*

People want to be led. If you can wrap your arms around that little fact, you will be a much better leader. Don't believe me? Let's look at some extreme examples in history: Hitler, Mao, Stalin, Pol Pot. All are proven mass murderers, yet you can still find large groups of people who yearn for the "good old days" of mind-numbing oppression and torture. How about Jim Jones? Good old Jim was the founder of the Peoples Temple, which moved to Jonestown, Guyana, in the seventies. On November 18, 1978, he somehow convinced more than nine hundred members of his church to commit mass suicide (they literally drank the Kool-Aid).

People want to be led...

Let's look at the power of the good side of leadership: George Washington at Valley Forge and throughout the Revolutionary War, Winston Churchill in the Battle of Britain, Ronald Reagan and the defeat of the Soviet Union in the Cold War. They are amazing examples of courage and leadership in the face of unbelievable odds, which changed the world for the better.

Good leadership is a trait that is hard to find these days. The PC movement has gotten to a point where people have become afraid to lead. Better not take that tough position because somebody might be offended and their self-esteem damaged! OMG!

Poor leadership can manifest in many ways that can cripple a business. The inability to fire an employee, taking too long to make a decision, and trying to make everybody happy are just a few examples. I know a business coach with a client who was afraid to come into the office because he was afraid of his office manager! I had a client who did not want to manage his people and was puzzled as to why his employees consistently did not live up to his expectations. Both of these companies were in dire straits financially. The lack of leadership was at the top of the list as the reason they were both in such difficult circumstances.

Most of the books for small business rightly advocate the importance of building process in a business. Unfortunately, many are left with the impression that good processes alone will guarantee a successful business. Good processes cannot overcome poor leadership, but good leadership can overcome poor processes.

There is no shortage of books on leadership. Some say that leadership can be taught. But others say it is an innate ability. Even if it can be taught, some have to work a lot harder at it than others. If you are overwhelmed and don't like what you are doing, you will not be a very good leader.

One day after losing a client, I asked myself why some of my clients were very successful working with me, and others were not. Once done beating myself up, I started looking at the ones who were successful. I noticed a common and important leadership trait: They all had the ability to get out of their own way.

What does that mean?

- They know they do not have all the answers.
- They are not too proud to ask for help or admit they do not know the answers.
- They seek out different perspectives from their own.
- They embrace change (some slower than others).
- And last, and most important, they can shelve their egos.

A great example of this happened to me. When I was the owner of a business coaching franchise, I put together a workshop series that we eventually took to multiple states. I lined up major newspapers, Chambers of Commerce, and other national businesses as sponsors. The plan was to use the workshop series to help acquire clients for other coaches and I would receive a percentage of that income. We had other organizations marketing and driving people to the workshops, and our marketing costs were very low. On paper, it was great. But in reality, I was getting very frustrated with the results of the program. So I did what most business owners do in situations like this; I put my head down and just worked harder, thinking I could fix it through brute force. (Pissed off a lot of people in the process…)

One day, my wife Barbara says to me, "You know, we are working harder than ever, but making less money than before we started this program…" BAM! Reality check! She was right, but it took me about a week to get my ego out of the way. Why a week? The program was my baby, and I had found out that there was a contingent who did not want the program to succeed. (Couldn't give them the satisfaction, could I?) Once I successfully pushed that ego monster back in its cave, I cancelled the program. We went back to making more money and not working as hard. Which by the way is one of my guiding principles: Make more money and don't work harder than you need to. It took an outside perspective to get me to see the obvious and get out of my own way.

However, be careful of where you are getting that perspective. I have seen numerous business owners take council from the very employees who are part of the problem. When I am hired to help turn around a company, I tell the business owner that if you do not have employees trying to get me fired, I am not doing my job. More often than not, you need an outside, unemotional, and unbiased perspective to help in the change process. Remember, most employees don't want you to get out of your own way – they like it just the way it is.

Another problem with some business owners is that they "act" like they want to change, but deep down they really don't because they are convinced they have all of the answers. "If I just keep doing what I am doing, it will eventually start working… Just a little longer… Oh crap, I am broke and out of business…"

I have had business owners request a meeting with me because they heard how I can help companies and then they proceed to tell me how great everything is working. One case in particular was a referral from a client. During our meeting, every potential issue I brought up was not a problem in his company. For example, his company had eight employees. He had turned over four of them in past six months, so I asked him what kind of a leader he thought he was. He looked at me quizzically and said something to the effect of: "It is not a leadership issue." So I asked him, "What kind of an issue is it?" He mumbled something about how they were just problem employees and he fixed that problem – and changed the subject. Finally, about one-and-a-half hours into the meeting, I bluntly asked him why he wanted to meet with me if everything was so great. He stuttered for a second before blurting out that he just could not do everything anymore and he was feeling out of control. He knew he needed to change but he was just unwilling to get out of his own way. He was more interested in finding somebody who would validate his opinion instead of actually making the necessary changes to grow his business.

CHAPTER 14

YOUR LEADERSHIP ABILITY WILL
MAKE OR BREAK YOUR COMPANY...

I think Smithers picked me because of my motivational skills...
Everyone says they have to work a lot harder when I'm around.
~ Homer Simpson

By the time most business owners start reaching out for help, they have some or all of the following problems:
- Losing money
- Sales are down, flat, or non-existent.
- The owner is working too many hours and is completely burned out.
- High employee turnover
- Not sure what to do next

We live in a society where we look for quick fixes everywhere and there is no accountability – "Not my fault!" I don't know how many times I have heard a business owner say something like: "My sales are down and I can't seem to keep good employees..." When pressed as to why they think they are in this situation, I get answers like:
- It's the economy.
- The competition is giving away their products.
- It is impossible to find good employees.

Rarely do I hear answers like:
- I must be doing something wrong but I just don't know what it is.
- I should probably take another look at my overall strategy

(or get one).
• I probably need to change my style of leadership.

I have found that the problem is usually looking at us in the mirror – start there first before looking for others to blame. Start there and you can fix your business, because your business is a direct reflection of you.

It is my belief that strong leadership is one of the single most important components in running a business. Unfortunately, poor leaders far outnumber good leaders. Most of these poor leaders do not even recognize in which category they fit. Like bad drivers, they complain about all the "other" bad drivers. I have never met a leader who admits to being part of the problem. Lack of self-awareness leads to self-deception. Self-awareness is one of the most important traits of a good leader.

A good leader sets the tone and the culture of the business. The leader creates a workplace where employees want to come to work. I know a business coach with a client who owned a restaurant. One of the reasons he hired the business coach was that he just did not understand why he had such high employee turnover. Seems his style of leading when it got really busy was to scream and yell at everybody. Imagine his shock when the coach pointed out that most people don't like to be yelled at, and that was probably one of the reasons he had such high turnover. He just thought it was really hard to find good employees and was looking for a better hiring process. Probably not very high on the self-awareness chart…

Attitude is everything. It has been said that leadership is the ability to hide panic from others and it is so true. I have seen so many business owners remain incredibly ignorant about their role in the mood of the company on a daily basis. Do your employees look to see if you close the door first thing in the morning? "Uh oh, is he is a bad mood *again*?" This is not good leadership.

If you are concerned about making payroll, do you let your employees know? NO! They will not hear that you are "concerned." What they will "hear" is that the company is "in trouble" and "we are all out of a job." Learn to keep your mouth shut.

If you have not done so already, take a behavioral assessment. You need to understand who you are, why you react the way you do and how you communicate. If you do nothing else suggested in this book – do this. Good ones only cost between one- to two-hundred dollars. So there is no excuse – unless you are afraid of what the results might be. Hire a professional who can give you candid feedback and won't gloss over the rough spots. And while you are at it – give your employees a behavioral assessment as well. You will be amazed at what you will learn. Suddenly you will understand why Becky can't shut-up and Bud just can't seem to get to those reports you keep asking for.

    This is the first place to start if you want to grow your business.

CHAPTER 15

Okay, Mr. Vince Lombardi... Now What Do I Do?

Leadership is a potent combination of strategy and character.
But if you must be without one, be without the strategy.
~ General Norman Schwarzkopf

Instead of rehashing the wisdom from all of the leadership books I have read, I will keep this simple.

First, stop making things so hard; this is hard enough as it is. This means for you and those around you. Give your employees the latitude to do things their way. You do not have all of the answers. There is ALWAYS somebody smarter than you. Who knows? You may get lucky and hire one.

Find out what works for you – know your limitations and shelve your ego. Figure out what you do best and enjoy – and outsource the rest.

The best leadership refresher I had in a long time came when I started coaching my son's soccer team. From that experience, I put together what I learned from ten nine-year-old soccer players.

Nine Leadership lessons from a team of nine-year-olds

I grew up playing soccer in California. A couple of years after my son started playing soccer, I caught the bug again. I kind of forgot I was not a teenager anymore and, at the young age of forty-seven, joined an over-thirty men's outdoor soccer league. The first year was very successful for my doctors, as my injuries mounted. They included a broken shoulder, a broken finger, a sprained ankle, and too many muscle pulls to count. After my son began watching me play, he asked if I would be the coach for his team. Since I am a business consultant, I figured: "How hard could this be?" The last thing I expected was a refresher course in leadership.

A little about the team and the league we play in: It is a "developmental" league and each team has ten players. Every child *has* to play two quarters. We don't keep score, and there are no standings. At the end of the season, each player gets a trophy – regardless of the outcome or the players' attitudes.

The team demographics were a slice of modern-day America and could just as easily be the roster of any company with ten employees. We had one boy from Pakistan who had never played soccer; we had two Hispanic boys with language and cultural issues. We had two boys from recently divorced families, and the emotional toll was apparent. Ironically, these two boys could not get along with each other. We had one boy whose skill level was two to three times higher than our average players, yet his father put lots of pressure on him to do better. We had another boy who was even better (when his head was in it). A couple of the boys clearly did not want to be there. This was their parents' efforts to get the kid some exercise and away from the video games. I applaud those parents for taking the initiative. In essence, the team was made up of boys with varying levels of skill and behavioral issues. Some of these issues were just typical of nine-year-old boys, and others were clearly issues related to their home environments – not much different than some of the companies I've run. But I did not realize that at the start of the season.

1. Set clear goals and expectations up-front.

One of the boys from the divorced family did not follow directions very well and it was obvious that there was not much discipline at home. At the beginning of the season it was always a chore to get him to follow directions. One day, we started doing a drill and he didn't pay attention (as usual). Actually, he was just the worst offender. Have you ever tried to get ten nine-year-old boys to all pay attention at once? They have the attention spans of gnats. Anyway, I was frustrated and finally told him to give me ten push-ups since he could not follow directions. He calmly looked at me and said "No."

Now remember, this is a "developmental" league. I could not cut his playing time because I *had* to play him. What power did I have? His mother was watching (so smacking him was not an option…) What to do?

It suddenly dawned on me that I had not properly set the rules and the clear expectations of the outcome if they did not follow the rules. So I turned to the team and said, "From this point forward, if you do not pay attention and follow the rules, you have to give me ten push-ups." To my surprise, EVERYBODY just said "okay" and started doing the drill.

Lessons Learned?
- In the absence of rules, people make up their own.
- Your employees cannot read your mind. While it may be painfully obvious to you what needs to be done, never assume they have the same perspective or initiative. Remember the "See Spot Run" books? Keep it that simple and spelled out.
- Are you setting clear expectations for your employees?
- Is it clearly understood what the outcome will be if they fail to meet those expectations?

2. Know what bar is being used to measure success.

One of my best players was a naturally talented soccer player. When his head was in the game, he could score five or more goals without trying real hard. He was that much better than most of the other players on the field.

In one game he had already scored four or five goals when I noticed he started pulling up on obvious shots and passing the ball away. At the next practice I asked his father why he had been pulling up on his shots. His response surprised me. The conversation went something like this:

> Me: "Why was Tim (alias) pulling up on his shots on Saturday?
> Father: "You noticed that?"
> Me: "Yeah, why was he doing that?"
> Father: "Well, I did not want him scoring too much…"
> Me: "Why?"
> Father: "I did not want it to look bad that he was scoring too

much. I thought it might make the other coaches or players mad."

Me: "The worst thing you can do for Tim is to stifle his ability. Do not make him play at a lower level just to compensate for those around him. If anything, you need to move him up to the Select league next year. Let him score as much as he can and don't inhibit his natural talent."

Father: "Really? What about the other coaches?"

Me: "Worry about your son, not the other coaches."

Lessons Learned?
- Are you stifling the abilities of the best players on your team so they won't make you or the weaker players look bad?
- Make the team play up to the ability of the best players, not down to the average players.

3. Most people want to do the right thing; don't assume they know what that is...

I mentioned earlier about one particular boy from a divorced home where discipline was not practiced with any regularity. He had a particularly rough week at practice. He was disrespecting his mother on the sideline and he was not doing a very good job of listening to me, either.

On game day, he came running up to me before the game and asked/demanded that he play goalie. I pulled him over to the side, away from the other players, got down on one knee so I was looking him straight in the eyes and said, "No, you disrespected your mother this week during practice and you disrespected me. When you can learn to change your behavior, I will put you in goal."

I expected him to melt down and start whining. Instead, he got this quizzical look on his face like: "Wow, I never thought of that before." He thought for a moment and then looked at me and just said, "Okay," and went back to the bench with the other players. He was not mad. Frankly, I was stunned. Then it dawned on me – there are probably no consequences to his actions in his life off of the soccer field. From that point forward, dealing with him became much easier. Oh, he still had his moments, but he really changed his behavior once he knew "the rules."

Lessons Learned?
- It is amazing what people think is acceptable behavior in an office. They assume what they are doing is okay since they do not know otherwise. I have had to speak to employees about personal hygiene and what we thought was their phobia to deodorant. I still remember the stunned looks on their faces when they realized what they were doing was not acceptable.
- Never assume a person's actions are just a flagrant disregard for the rules. They honestly may not know any better.
- Be careful when "correcting" the behavior. You do not want to belittle or embarrass the employee for something they may consider to be "normal."

4. Winning is contagious.

Early in the season, I found the outcome of the first quarter was very important to the tone of the rest of the game. If we were "winning" after the first quarter, the team played with more confidence and was more upbeat for the rest of the game. So much in fact, that I started building my lineup with my best players to start the game.

The first game of the season, we got clobbered. Clobbered right out of the box and it was not pretty. Our two best players were not at the game and we did not have a lot of time to practice. And it was hot, very hot. At one point during the game I looked at the opposing team on the sideline and saw that the boys were playing chase around the bench. I looked at my players and they were huddled under an umbrella trying to get out of the sun, whining about how hot it was. That was embarrassing.

Later in the season we played the same team and by this time we were consistently winning. However, our team was anxious because they vividly remembered the outcome of the first game. We jumped out to an early lead and their confidence soared. They seemed to forget about the first game and went on to win.

Lessons Learned?
- Get early wins and celebrate.
- Winning is contagious, but so is losing.
- Winners are attracted to a winning culture and winning leadership.

5. Everybody keeps score.

As this was a developmental league, we did not keep score. As coaches we were told not to focus on the score but to emphasize development and let the kids have fun. I have always been very competitive so I was struggling with this concept of not keeping score. Keeping score seemed to me to be the whole point.

What I quickly discovered was that EVERYBODY was keeping score – the kids, the parents on the sideline, and the coaches. Even the referees were keeping track of which kids scored. In fact, my kids were coming up to me and telling me they played this team last year and the final score of that game.

During one game we were getting beat at half-time and I was trying to emphasize having fun over the score. At one point during my half-time speech, one of my players said, "Forget fun; losing sucks!" So much for my half-time speech...

The boys also kept score on who were the "best" players on the team. They kept score on who did not show up to all of the practices and games. They kept scores of their past coaches and whether they played favorites with the players, especially if the coach's son was on the team. They kept score on everything!

Lessons Learned?
- Your team of employees does the same thing. They keep score of everything.
- Make sure you are keeping score of positive things, not negative things. Things that keep up morale and not the things that bring morale down.
- Keeping score does matter as it gives the team a goal and a rallying point.

6. Don't play favorites.

Unfortunately, it is human nature – we like some people better than others. As a leader, we have to be cognizant of whether we are playing favorites. Since my son is on the team, there is the natural tendency to place him first. But you can't; it undermines the team. I am pleased to say I have never been accused of playing favorites on my son's team. My son's teammates look at him as another player, not the coach's son. This is the best thing I could have done for him.

I made sure everybody had a chance to play captain. If I forgot who was captain last time, they would let me know – loudly. The team knew I would be fair and expected me to act accordingly. In fact, they helped keep me honest.

Playing favorites in the workplace is one of the best ways to destroy a team – "She only got that promotion because the boss likes her;" or "It is only because his father is the president that he got away with that; if that was me, I would have been fired in a second." You probably will not hear those comments, but they will be said.

Lessons Learned?
- Playing favorites lowers the perception of that person by their peers.
- They WILL notice.
- If you are a family-owned business with family as employees, you have this problem. Trust me; you do.

7. Be aware of outside influences.

Of my ten players, some parents could never figure out how to be at practice or games on time. Others were punctual and, if they could not make it or they were going to be late, they would let me know. It is unfortunate that this simple act of courteousness was the exception, not the rule.

As the season went along, the boys were getting to a point where they did not want to let me down. The boys from the troubled families seemed to be at the top of that list. One Saturday we had a game that started at one o'clock. One of these boys showed up late and walked over to me all dejected, embarrassed, and feeling responsible for the situation.

Our conversation went something like this:

Nine-year-old: "Sorry I am late, coach"

Me: "Why? Were you driving?"

Nine-year-old: "Huh? No, I wasn't driving!"

Me: "Then I guess you have nothing to be sorry for; do you?"

He thinks about this for a minute and then his face lights up when he realized I was not going to be angry with him, and he says, "My mom stayed out late last night and just got up…". Too much information – so

I quickly changed the subject…

Sometimes I am not too optimistic about the human race. We can really do some stupid things and think they were acts of genius. How many times have you seen somebody do something of questionable intellect and said, "What was he thinking?" More often than not, they did it because of some outside influence: to impress somebody, for revenge or just to get noticed. Employees' outside influences will be brought into the office. Count on it. Don't think they can separate the two – especially if drugs or alcohol are involved.

Lessons Learned?

- Sometimes things happen that are out of the employees' control. Be sensitive to this when it happens. Just don't let the behaviors become a habit.
- Your employees' moods can and will be influence by events prior to their arrival at the office. Let's suppose a husband had a fight with his wife prior to getting to work and arrives already in a bad mood. Do you really think launching in on him about being five minutes late is going to motivate him to do better? No, it will not. This is one of the reasons the expression "going postal" has become part of our cultural lexicon.

8. Provide feedback – in a positive way.

One day my son brought up the actions of one of his coaches from two years earlier. I thought the coach was pretty good, considering he was trying to corral a bunch of seven-year-olds.

I had heard him give positive encouragement on numerous occasions. But it turns out that during a game, when the parents were on the other side of the field and couldn't hear, he would deliver some very harsh criticisms of the team's play. This would occur between each quarter of play. I don't know exactly what he said but what my nine-year-old son remembered, filtered through the ears of a seven-year-old, was: "You guys are horrible; you don't deserve to win." Even when they scored a goal, he sometimes said they were just lucky and needed to play harder. Now he may not have even said that, but that is what my son remembers.

My son did not remember all of the positive words of

encouragement; he only remembered the bad. Accordingly, he remembered the coach as being horrible and did not like playing for him.

I was adamant that I would not make the same mistake. That is not to say I did not feel like saying things like that out of frustration, but good leaders keep such things to themselves. As I stated before, one definition of leadership is the ability to hide panic from others.

I had a boy on my team who was his own worst critic. Coincidentally, he was one of the boys from the divorced family. He was consistently one of my best players but he always thought he played poorly. In one game he did have a bad first quarter. He came off the field in tears. "I suck, Coach!" was his common refrain. I pulled him aside and talked about what he did right that quarter, not what he did wrong. I put him back in the game with the advice: "I think you did fine, but if you think you played so bad last quarter, go out there and play hard and make up for it." He went back out there and played great – he was on a mission.

At the end of the season, his father thanked me for taking the time to coach and said his son really enjoyed playing for me and he looked forward to practices and the games. He said that playing soccer this year had really helped keep him grounded, which was important because of the family situation. It is times like that when you remember why you volunteer your time to coach the kids in the first place.

Some of my best memories from coaching that season came from the players who were not natural talents. I would point out what they were doing right and coach them in positive ways on the areas they needed to improve. When they would do something right for the first time on the field, they always looked over to make sure I saw what they had done. I yelled out congratulations and their faces just beamed.

Lessons Learned?

- As an adult, think about how many times a day that you receive positive feedback. For most people, it is very rare. More often than you would think, the only good words most will hear are at work. They get more than enough negative feedback from their families and life circumstances. I once had a woman working for me whose home life was so bad that work was a place to get away.
- I am not a big advocate of annual reviews. I believe that if you

are leading and managing your people effectively, you don't need an annual review, as they will already know how they are doing. You can say ninety-nine positive things about an employee during a review and one negative, and all they will remember is the one negative comment.

- I had a client who was concerned about the "professionalism" of "casual Fridays." One woman in particular had a tendency to wear some rather revealing clothes that the owner felt were inappropriate. The owner's first reaction was that he wanted to tell her to stop dressing like a slut (his words…). Instead of a frontal assault, we decided that the best course of action was to provide the team with polo shirts with the company logo on the front and make that the "dress code" on Fridays. Jeans were still acceptable. He rolled out the new dress code and the woman who had prompted the whole discussion was the first to express her delight. She thought it was a great idea! Totally different outcome.
- Words matter; choose them carefully.

9. Don't be afraid to lead.

After the first couple of practices, I realized that I had no real control or power over these kids and that I better not let them realize the truth of the situation. At first I did something that was not a natural act for me: I shrunk from my leadership responsibilities. Coincidently, we lost our first two games. The next practice, I started being their leader again and we went on to win our next seven games. Did we lose those first two games because I did not step up? We will never know, but I do believe that it played a factor.

In my leadership seminars, I ask the audience to describe "leadership." Leadership turns out to be a very difficult concept to define. But you know it when you see it.

Some people associate leadership with conflict. My opinion is that good leadership actually reduces conflict. People want and need to be led. They will gladly turn over the reins to a leader they trust and believe in.

Leadership does not mean that you are a "friend." You cannot lead and make everybody happy. As Margaret Thatcher said, "Consensus is the absence of leadership."

SECTION III

SALES

CHAPTER 16

ONLY THE STRONG WILL SURVIVE...

We're adding a little something to this month's sales contest.
As you all know, first prize is a Cadillac Eldorado.
Anybody want to see second prize?
Second prize is a set of steak knives.
Third prize is you're fired.
~ Blake in *Glengarry Glen Ross*, 1992

In an economic meltdown, you will need the best sales reps, the best messaging, and the best sales processes if you are to be among the last still standing. It does not suffice to merely answer the phone or have mediocre sales reps trying to sell in spite of themselves. You need to be aggressive – but not obnoxiously aggressive. You need to help a competitor go out of business by luring away his customers and best employees. If you don't do it to them, they will do it to you. You need to show up at a knife fight with a gun.

With fewer buying customers and more desperate competitors, competitor strategies will be to cut prices and reduce services. Some competitors may already be dead, but don't yet know it. They are just living off cash flow, racking up the debt. I think the polite thing to do is put them out of their misery a little sooner. Don't you?

"Sales" is the reason for business; without sales there is no business. That seems obvious, but the majority of business owners do not like sales. Numerous business owners have told me that they don't like sales because:

- I don't want to be pushy.
- I don't like to be asked these kinds of questions.
- I don't want to make them mad.

I was teaching consultative questioning to the sales team for a client. One of the reps was clearly uncomfortable with my message. When I asked him why, he replied: "I don't like people asking me those questions so I won't do it to them." Mind you, these were questions like: "How much is your budget?" Not, "Can I borrow your car?" The context of the questions did not matter; he just did not like to be asked questions. After the meeting I recommended to the owner that he either fire this rep or move him out of sales, because he was not going to be successful.

In my workshops and seminars, I ask, "What is the first thing that comes to mind when I say salesman?" I always get answers like: sleazy, dishonest, and pushy. Are you projecting your beliefs into the sales cycle? If you are like most people, you probably are.

I then ask the group; "How many of you are in sales?" I have yet to get everybody in the room to raise their hands. If you are in business, you are in sales. If you are in a relationship, you are in sales. Everybody in your company is in sales. For those of you uncomfortable with sales, you had better get your head around this if you want your business to be successful. If you don't like sales, then hire somebody who does...

A logical solution to this problem would be education and training. I searched one of the top Internet book resellers for "sales" and came up with 671,129 choices. 671,129! Assuming that at least some of these books are helpful, you would think the failure rate of small business would be somewhere south of fifty percent, instead of the high rate of failure that actually exists. So what gives? Nobody reading these books? Or maybe it is just the same small group of people reading all of the books? Nobody really knows, but it is obvious something is not working.

How about sales training? Surely that works. Right? *Wrong*. Most of the time it does not work, either. Following are some of the bedrocks of traditional sales training:

- You need to sell the benefits of your product(s).
- A sales rep should have a canned pitch.
- There is a "sales personality."
- A sales rep should have a closing script.
- Enthusiasm is the key to a successful sales pitch.

- Having a big Rolodex is an indicator of future success.
- A sales rep should use qualifying questions.
- Selling is a numbers game.
- Close early and close often.
- Never attack the competition.
- Always call high in the organization.
- Every NO leads to a YES.
- You have to be good at handling rejection in order to be successful in sales.

Every single one of these points is taught as the truth in a sales training class somewhere. Yet if you do a search on the Internet, you can find these same bullet points referenced as sales myths by sales training companies. So which one is it? Let's pick one of the items in the list. Is enthusiasm the key to a successful sales pitch? No, it is not THE key, but it is *a* key. People like passion. Given the choice of buying the same product from Joe Boring or Suzy Enthusiasm, most people will choose Suzy every time.

If you are not the enthusiastic kind, can you be taught to behave enthusiastically and still be genuine? Probably not. My public speaking style is very direct and to the point. I am not a "rah rah" type of speaker. If I tried to be "rah rah," it would fall flat with the audience. Why? Because it would not be genuine. So, can sales training help you learn this trait and use it effectively? I think not. If you are a good salesperson, you probably just do what comes naturally, regardless of what you might have heard in a sales training class.

Bottom line is this: If you are not comfortable in sales, you better hire a sales rep. If you cannot afford to hire a sales rep, you better start doing some serious work on yourself to learn how to become better at sales. Will you ever become a "natural" salesperson? The odds are against it. There is a reason some people like finance or operations; it is how they are wired. It is the same reason good salespeople do not like operations; that is how they are wired.

As I stated earlier, I was part of an organization of business coaches. With a couple of exceptions, the most successful coaches were those with a sales background. Not operations, not human resources. You would think that somebody with twenty-five years in HR would probably make a good coach. After all, they like to help people. The problem is they have to know how to close the sale before they can help the customer. They never get a chance to help the customer because they keep striking out when they try to close the deal. I guess they don't want to seem pushy...

You can learn sales tactics all day long, but if you are fundamentally uncomfortable with the process, you simply will not do it. There is an author on the speaking circuit who has a book about creating a sales machine. One of his war stories is how he called the president of a company so many times that the president finally called him back to tell him to stop calling. And once he had him on the phone, and nine rejections later, he got the president to agree to a meeting and eventually got them as a client. You can't teach that kind of tenacity and you can't teach that ability to handle rejection. It is completely unrealistic to think you can teach somebody who does not like sales, either by reading a book or attending sales training, to change their behavior to act as if they do. To most people, calling one time and getting rejected is the psychological equivalent to being rejected nine times.

The best advice I can give you about sales is to forget all the "tactics" you have been taught. Just be yourself and ask questions. People still buy from people they like and people who are genuine. A lot of the tactics still being taught are from a different era. I just shake my head when I see somebody still promoting the idea of "the first person who speaks loses." This tactic is only supposed to be used once you ask the "closing" question. Once the question is asked, do not speak. I have heard sales reps brag that they sat there for twenty minutes without saying a word until their prospect broke and spoke first. Complete BS. The only thing this accomplishes is greatly increasing the chance for buyer's remorse. One of the top reasons for buyer's remorse is when the prospect felt they were pressured into a deal. These types of tactics might have worked in days gone by, but that is "ancient" history.

CHAPTER 17

MOST SALES TRAINING DOES NOT WORK...

Sales are contingent upon the attitude of the salesman –
not the attitude of the prospect.
~ W. Clement Stone

L et's take a closer look at sales training. Most sales training is based on
tactics such as closing techniques, overcoming objections, and getting
around gatekeepers. There are some very good tactics trainings and some
very bad. However, most training is dated and geared for a prospect that
no longer exists. The typical prospect these days is more cynical, less loyal,
and frankly, does not care.

One of my clients sent a sales rep to a training class that was
sponsored by the company whose software they resold. This training was
put together by one of the biggest software companies in the world. The
first problem was that there was way too much information to process.
The handout from the class was more than 130 double-sided pages. The
program supposedly taught reps how to build value, consultative selling
techniques, and how to build and foster an "internal coach." You name it;
they covered it. After taking 105 pages to train the reps to sell value, etc.,
the recommended closing technique was to offer the prospect a discount
if they signed today! Pathetic! All that training and the closing technique
is to offer a discount? *Gee,* nobody ever thought of that before...

But here is the kicker. At the beginning of the training, they have
a "talent" assessment. They categorize sales reps into two categories: Eagles
and Journey People. According to this assessment, only twenty percent of

sales reps are Eagles. The other eighty percent are Journey People. What makes a sales rep an Eagle is that they are intuitive, have conversations, and ask questions. Journey People make presentations, make statements, and process is the key to success. So in essence, twenty percent of sales reps are naturals and the other eighty percent have to follow a process in order to be successful. But if you look at a typical sales team, you will have the 80-20 rule in effect. Twenty percent of the reps are selling eighty percent of revenue. This twenty percent are the Eagles. It is because of these natural talents that they are successful, not because of process. And yet these Eagles are forced to sit through this inane training because... I am not sure why... maybe it is just lousy management.

Can you teach Journey People to be Eagles? How do you teach somebody to be intuitive and know when to ask the right questions during a conversation? You can't. A canned conversation will come off as canned, no matter how many times you role play. I guess when you look at the program through this lens, it makes even less sense, since the Journey People are going to resort to discounting to get the deal anyway.

Throughout my sales career, I have attended way too many sales training classes. And as a manager, I sent my teams to numerous training sessions. After a while, I noticed something interesting. At the end of training on Friday, the reps were ready to take on the world with their new-found knowledge. By the end of the next week they were starting to fall back into their old habits. After a couple of weeks, it is like the training never occurred. Why is that? My opinion: sales is all about psychology. The psychology of the seller and the buyer. The problem with most sales training is that it does not change the psychology of the seller. I can teach you the greatest techniques and tactics in the world, but if your personal psychology gets in the way, you will not use them. For example, if you do not like to ask closing questions because of a deep-rooted belief, you will not do so – regardless of the pressure put on you to ask these questions.

At one of the companies where I was the VP of sales, I was asked by one of our resellers to help a sales rep try to save a deal he had all but lost. The sales rep was stunned that he was going to lose the deal since the prospect "liked him so much." I spoke with the prospect and confirmed that he had decided on the other product but had just not signed the paperwork. He spoke very highly of our reseller's sales rep – "He is a very nice guy." Unfortunately, the sales rep got out-sold by somebody who was not quite as nice but did a better job of presenting a solution that met the prospect's need.

At that point, our only option was a Hail Mary pass that was either going to get us the deal or possibly anger the prospect. When I gave the sales rep my recommendation, his immediate response was: "I can't do that! That might make him mad and ruin our relationship! When they are ready to buy software again in another five years, I want him to buy from me but he won't if I make him mad now!" My only response was to ask him if he realized that what he said was spoken out loud.

His personal need to be liked completely overruled any business tactic or recommendation. By the way, he never tried the Hail Mary pass, and the other rep got the deal. But he and the prospect are probably still friends...

CHAPTER 18

WANT VS. NEED...

Bart, with $10,000, we'd be millionaires!
We could buy all kinds of useful things like... love!
~ Homer Simpson

Why do people buy? Why do they not buy? Why do some people spend more money on a car than their home is worth? Why do people buy designer clothes when they can buy something just like it without the label (probably made in the same factory) for much less? Why do people buy an Acura when a Honda Accord is just as reliable? One word: psychology.

Why do people buy your product or service? What emotional need does it meet? Is it status? How about comfort? Does it save them money or time? Do your customers associate pain or pleasure with your product or service? If you do not know, ask your customers. They will gladly tell you. You NEED to know.

If you live in the United States, chances are you "need" very little. We have the highest standard of living on the planet. But we "want" everything. I get angry when I hear people talk about the poverty in the United States. Poverty is Haiti. Poverty is Sudan. I am not disputing there are people in real need in our country. But there are a lot of people living below the "poverty line" with cell phones, TVs, and twenty-two-inch rims. You rarely see a malnourished poor person in the United States. In fact, quite a few need to drop some weight. You don't see an obesity problem in Haiti. That is where there is "need."

Know the difference and how it relates to your product and you will be one step closer to increasing revenue.

CHAPTER 19

SALES REPS... ARGH!

Yeah, I called her up; she gave me a bunch of crap about me not listening to her, or something, I don't know, I wasn't really paying attention.
~ Harry, *Dumb and Dumber*, 1994

Let me preface this chapter by reminding you I am a "sales guy." My first real sales job was selling computers in the eighties. I can remember when the IBM XT came out and it had a 10MB disk drive. We were all wondering what we were going to do with all that disk space. With that said, I feel like I am ratting on the brotherhood with this chapter...

Some "experts" are asking the question of why we even need salespeople. After all, I can get just about all of the product knowledge I need on the Internet or your website.

One of my clients recently purchased some software, in spite of the sales rep. If you were to ask the sales rep, I bet he would have a completely different story about how he "controlled the sales cycle" and "closed the deal." All complete bull. The only value the sales rep provided was setting up the demonstration and sending the paperwork for purchase, and he made that difficult. It was like the rep was going through a dance and was thinking he was leading my client around the dance floor. The problem was my client was not even in the building, let alone on the dance floor. The rep was out there dancing alone and had no clue. Yet I guarantee that the rep and his sales manager were high-fiving each other for a job well done. My client was left with a bad taste in his mouth about the company because of his sales experience. Just on principle I wanted to call up the sales manager and let him know what a moron he has on staff, but I did not have a dog in that fight…

It is my opinion that one of the most expensive and frustrating mistakes a business owner can make is to hire the wrong sales rep. Unfortunately, it happens most of the time. Part of the reason is that most people do not like sales or salespeople. So when they go about hiring a sales rep, they hire somebody more like themselves than like a good sales rep. Another reason is that there is a real shortage of good salespeople. It is my belief that if you randomly took one hundred "salespeople," eighty of them should not be in sales, and ten are selling the wrong product. The remaining ten are selling the right product with the right skill set. And that might be a little generous…

Managing salespeople brings its own joy to your world. Be prepared, very prepared. Good salespeople are aggressive, ambitious, often arrogant and, most of the time, strong-willed. They don't listen very well and they are not detail oriented. They disdain paperwork and require a strong leader. *Damn!* There is that leadership thing again!

When I was a VP of sales, the COO came to me shortly after I started and said he wanted me to build a team of type-A sales reps and he was willing to pay the appropriate six-figure compensation. As luck would have it, I knew of a type-A who was about to change jobs (he worked for me at another company) so I called him and convinced him to come work for us. This rep was great and always over quota.

A couple of weeks after he started, the COO came into my office and we had a conversation that went something like this:

COO: I am concerned about some of the things I am hearing about Tom (not his real name).

Me: "Like what?"

COO: "Well, I hear he is a little arrogant…"

Me: "Yep, he is…"

He gave me a dumbfounded look and walked out of my office.

A week later he was back in my office to tell me he is hearing that Tom does not listen very well. I responded that this observation was true, which resulted in the same look from our previous conversation. Shortly after that he was back in my office, complaining that Tom did not follow directions very well. Of course, he was right. So I looked at him and said, "You want me to build a stable of type-A sales reps and you cannot handle one. Which way do you want it?"

He just shook his head and left.

The moral of the story is that good salespeople are worth their weight in gold and require a very different way to manage and motivate than somebody in operations or administration. Good sales reps like competition and recognition. They hate paperwork and are not very detail oriented. They like to be rewarded for their efforts with no caps on their compensation. It is not uncommon for good salespeople to make more money than the president of the company. You want it this way; it is a good thing. It amazes me to see business owners feeling resentful about the amount of money their sales reps are making. If the comp plan for your reps is profitable for the company, then get over it. Chances are you could not have sold as much as they did anyway.

Hire right the first time. I have been in sales for over thirty years, so I am not speaking out of turn when I say: be very wary of what you hear during an interview with a sales rep. In all of the interviews I have done with prospective salespeople, I can count on one hand the number who admitted they were not over one hundred percent of quota. It seems every sales rep has been at one hundred percent quota their entire career. I will let you in on a little secret… salespeople might lie during an interview. Just a warning…

If you are not good at hiring salespeople, use a recruiter. A good one will save you time and money. If sales reps are not paying for themselves and making you a profit, change the comp plan or fire them – quick. In these economic times, there is way too much talent on the street looking for work to be stuck with a "C" player.

One of the perennial problems for small-business owners is that they could not afford "A" and "B" quality salespeople. There is a reason some reps are six-figure sales reps and others make $30K. They are better – plain and simple. Economic circumstances may offer the opportunity for small-business owners to hire six-figure sales reps without paying six-figures for the talent. Upgrade, upgrade, upgrade.

CHAPTER 20

TEN-DOLLAR SOLUTION TO A FIVE-DOLLAR PROBLEM...

Every sale has five basic obstacles: no need, no money, no hurry, no desire, no trust.
~ Zig Ziglar

B ack in the eighties, I decided to start a software company with a friend of mine. Yes, I have done it, too. We were offering solutions to the moving and storage industry. After talking with LOTS of moving and storage companies and listening to them complain about costs, we determined that a program that tracks packing material would be the first program we'd develop. We had LOTS of people tell us they would buy the program if we developed it. So we did what every dumb-ass budding entrepreneur does; we quit our jobs and started our own software company. After all, LOTS of people wanted it! We did the projections on a spreadsheet to see just how rich we were going to be; life was going to be good!

Once we developed the software, we found out that it was really impractical to track these materials. It actually cost more money in labor to track the materials than it did to just live with the loss. *DOH! How did we miss that?*

Turns out our survey of LOTS of people was not enough. It was just what we wanted to hear. It was a painful lesson as we had to fold up shop and get jobs.

Lessons learned?

- Just because you have a great idea does not mean that people will buy it, even if they say they will.
- Be careful about drawing a conclusion based on a survey of one (or LOTS).
- Don't start a business unless you can afford to suffer through your first defeats. We only had enough funds to take one shot...

On the other hand, people will buy completely useless stuff. Remember the Pet Rock? There is no accounting for how humans will behave. All sales are emotionally based. We use logic to justify our decisions. Be very honest about the need for your product. Just because you like it does not mean others will.

CHAPTER 21

COMPETING WITH WAL-MART...

All right, let's not panic. I'll make the money by selling one of my livers.
I can get by with one.
~ Homer Simpson

Why is Wal-Mart so successful? Because their prices are low and they have a huge selection. It is not the best stuff, nor is it the worst stuff. Just the stuff that "most" people want to buy. Oh yeah, and I can pick up some milk while I am there, too...

I am still amazed to find people who want to get into a business that has Wal-Mart as a direct competitor. Yet they have no idea how to differentiate themselves from the eight-hundred-pound gorilla in the room. If you are thinking about picking that fight, understand you cannot win on price or quantity of selection. However, you can compete on quality, uniqueness and, maybe, location. Some people don't mind paying twice as much for a gallon of milk when they pick up their cigarettes at the convenience store.

Wal-Mart has been vilified for destroying small businesses in every town in which they set up shop. While I sympathize with the owners of these businesses, nobody is forcing their customers to shop at Wal-Mart. They CHOOSE to shop there. Is that Wal-Mart's fault? Nope. It just means they have a better offering than the competitors in the area. The protesters cry, "But it will kill downtown!" If downtown does not have something to offer other than being "downtown," that will be true.

So if you are selling the same product(s) as Wal-Mart, you better be cheaper (impossible) or more convenient (doubtful, they are just about everywhere), or provide a better shopping experience (See Target). If you are none of the above, it is time for plan "B."

CHAPTER 22

THE BAR IS SET REALLY LOW...

Equal opportunity means everyone will have a fair chance at being incompetent.
~ Laurence J. Peter

The good news when competing with most of the big-box stores is that customer service really sucks. They seem to go out of their way to piss off their customers.

My Xbox 360 went into the infamous "three red rings of death" crash. I happened to buy the service plan for the 360 because I had heard of this problem and I did not want to be without Halo for six weeks while it was shipped off to be repaired (note: emotional reason for purchasing the service plan). The plan would simply swap out the box for a new one. Cool...

I called up the big-box store (the blue one, not the red one, which is now out of business) to find out what I needed to do to exchange the 360. The customer service rep informs me that my plan only covers sending the box off for repair. I politely point out that this is not the case; it is for a swap. I ask him to pull up my info on their system so he can verify. He says he has my info and proceeds to debate with me about whether my plan is for swapping the 360 or sending it away to be repaired. When I asked him why I would purchase a plan that does the same thing I could do without a plan, he seemed to not understand the finer points of my argument. So I let him know he was a moron and asked him to put a manager on the phone or somebody who has a clue. Imagine my surprise when I get put into voicemail jail with no chance of parole. So after waiting on hold for a very long time, I hang up. *Must have been my tone...* Anyway, I call back two more times to the service department and now nobody will answer the phone. *It never occurred to me they might have caller ID...*

So out of frustration, I gather up my 360 and head over to the big blue box. The service department has a huge line of other pissed-off customers and the line is not moving. There are only two service reps waiting on customers. One of the customers does not have a clue about computers and is trying to learn everything about Vista while debating the rep on why his hard drive crashed. Blind leading the blind. The other rep was trying to communicate with a family that did not speak English very well. The only person with somewhat of a grasp on the English language was the teenage son. From what I could tell, they were either trying to swap or fix an Apple laptop that did not have a serial number – most likely a bootleg system. Seems the teenage son did understand the importance of a serial number but could not pass along the information in a manner that made sense to the father. They went round and round as the line got longer. Meanwhile back in line, the natives were getting restless. Countless other employees were walking by this line and not doing a thing to help ease our pain. So I started asking employees to bring me a manager. It took three times before a manager showed up. Suddenly, two additional reps became available (after the manager showed up). Amazing. Why did it take me getting a manager before they put extra people on the line? "Not my job, man."

I finally got to speak with a rep. He pulled up my info and immediately verified the plan was for a swap. What was the first guy reading? Turns out I forgot one of the cables back at the house – and they could not swap out the box unless they had the cable. I recommended they just go get the 360 they were going to swap with me and take the cable out of the box. Noooo, that would be too simple and it was against the rules. Once again, I called for the manager. He proceeded to tell me that the blue-box store's entire relationship with Microsoft would be in jeopardy if he took the cable from the box. By this time, I was blowing a fuse. I was ripping this guy a new one about customer service and is this any way to treat a customer when he offered me a gift card for my inconvenience. I still had to go home and get the old cable, but now I had a gift card. Yeah! The manager leaves to go brilliantly solve another customer crisis. As I was given the gift card, I asked how much it is worth. Beaming, the customer service rep responded, "Ten dollars!" With the best tone I could muster, my reply was something along the line of: "You have got to be kidding me...ten dollars?

Woo hoo! Ten bucks, that sure made me happy and I forgot about the whole situation... except when I tell the story in my seminars, public speaking engagements, and this book...

Bottom line: The truth is that these big-box stores are mostly filled with blind robots as employees following idiot rules. Because of this perfect storm of mediocrity, you are going to get bad service from employees who don't care. And unfortunately, this problem is not limited to the big-box stores. It is everywhere.

If you can't compete with this level of service, rethink your whole business model. Great customer service will help differentiate you in the marketplace. Fortunately it is not that hard to do. Now finding the employees who give a $#!%... well, read the section on employees and you will understand.

CHAPTER 23

OKAY, MR. HERB TARLEK... NOW WHAT DO I DO?

We made too many wrong mistakes.
~ Yogi Berra

Type "sales" into Amazon.com and you will find hundreds of thousands of books from which to select. There are secrets and "ultimate" secrets to selling more. There are strategies and ultimate strategies. There is SPIN selling, consultative selling, and quid pro quo selling. There are fifty rules, sixteen rules, and seven rules to sell more. There are five steps, twenty-five habits, 12.5 principles, forty-nine principles, six keys, twenty-one ways, fifty ways, and a hundred-and-one strategies for becoming an awesome sales rep. So many books on sales, and yet most salespeople suck. Go figure.

What to do? I had a sales rep tell me once that sales is the easiest job in the world when done incorrectly and hardest when done correctly. Even after being in sales for more than thirty years, I am still learning. So, let's just keep this simple.

We use emotions to make a buying decision, and logic to justify it. Why do people spend ten thousand dollars on a Rolex watch when a thirty-dollar Casio will keep just as good (or better) time? It is emotion that makes the decision. Houses, cars, shoes, you name it, and all are emotion-based buying decisions. Why is your customer buying now and not six months ago? Or six months from now? What happens if they do nothing? Who is the real buyer? One of my clients sold vans for people in wheelchairs. When we started looking at the sales process and developing questions to ask the prospect, we discovered something very important: more often than not the real customer was the spouse of the person in the wheelchair. It was not the handicapped person! Why? Because it was the spouse that had to do all of the heavy lifting and pushing to get their partner in and out of their existing vehicle. With these vans, the person in the wheelchair can drive right in with no lifting required of the spouse. Often we found that the person in the wheelchair was satisfied with the current situation and did not see a reason to change. Who is the *REAL* buyer of your product?

So just focus on learning to ask questions that uncover the emotional reason your prospect is buying, and then shut up and listen. If you don't like asking questions, you are not going to do very well in sales.

The Sales Cycle

Every sale follows a cycle. The time spent in each stage will vary depending on the product or service, but there is a process. The problem with most sales is that people fail to follow the cycle in the proper order. Here is my version of the universal stages of every sales cycle (in order):

1. **Suspect:** This is a potential consumer of your product.
2. **Lead/Prospect:** This is a potential consumer who has expressed an interest in your product.
3. **Qualify:** This is where you find out the basic questions such as – When does the prospect want to buy? How much is in the prospect's budget? Do you have the right product to meet their needs?
4. **Discovery:** It is during this stage that you need to find out the emotional reasons (pain or pleasure) the prospect is interested in buying your goods or services. Why are they buying? Why now? What happens if they don't buy? What happens if they make the wrong decision?
5. **Solution/Presentation:** It is during this stage that you show the prospect how your goods and services can meet the needs of the prospect.
6. **Negotiation:** This stage is where you reach final agreement on things like price, terms, delivery, etc.
7. **Close:** You get a signed contract or are paid.

Most salespeople will skip the two most important steps in the process: the qualifying stage and discovery stage, and go straight to the solution/presentation stage. "Brochure dump" and "Show up and throw up" are just a couple of the terms to describe this act of sales self-destruction. It is easy to spot because most salespeople are guilty of some version of the brochure dump as it goes something like this...

A sales rep gets a call from "somebody" who has "questions" about their product. Because they are so excited to have a live body on the other end of the phone, they immediately start talking about all the great features of their widget. They skip the qualify and discovery stage because they don't want to find out the prospect has no money and no real need, or twenty other reasons that might kill the sale. (If they hope hard enough, that little problem might disappear on its own. Why bring it up?) So in their excitement to close the deal, they jump straight to solution/presentation and start blasting the prospect with a barrage of features. This is usually followed by the prospect asking, "How much does it cost?" BAM – straight to price, do not pass go, let the negotiations begin!

Ironically, ask ten salespeople what stage(s) cause them the most stress, and they will tell you it is the stages of negotiation and close (if they answer honestly). Why? Because most people associate these stages with conflict. Since they have not created any emotional connection or reasons for the prospect to buy, the prospect focuses on one thing: price. And because they skipped the qualifying and discovery stages, they are now in a price negotiation, which is the very stage that stresses them out in the first place.

So now the sales cycle looks like this:

1. **Suspect**
2. **Lead / Prospect**
3. **Solution/Presentation:** This becomes a brochure dump because the sales rep does not know the emotional reasons the prospect is using for making the purchase.
4. **Negotiation:** This negotiation becomes focused on price because there is no other point on which to focus.
5. **Close:** If the sales rep winds up closing the deal it is usually because they discounted the product. This sales strategy is a profit killer.
6. **Discovery / Qualify:** This is where the sales rep discovers the

prospect has no money or need, and has wasted three months chasing a deal that was not closing in the first place.

If you ask the right questions during the qualifying and discovery stages, the prospect will tell you the emotional reasons they are interested in buying your product. Often you will find that the prospect may have never even verbalized the reason they are buying. Getting them to say it for the first time can be very powerful. The prospect now thinks you "get" him or her and will want to buy from you because you are so smart.

Armed with this information, you can tailor your solution-presentation stage to meet the emotional needs of the buyer. Done properly, and assuming your product meets the needs of the prospect, the negotiation and close stages do not become the focus of the sales cycle. Often the prospect will close the deal themselves!

Customer service

No rocket science here; just don't screw with your customers. It is so simple, yet this notion seems to be incomprehensible to the majority of businesses and employees. It has turned into a viscous battle between employees and customers because customers now expect bad service and employees are more than happy to give it to them. It has become a self-fulfilling prophecy of mediocrity.

After having my truck serviced, I noticed the earphones for my iPhone were no longer on the passenger seat. I thought they had been stolen so I called and left a message for the service advisor and the service manager. The service advisor called me right back and I informed him that he may have a theft problem. He sounds more pissed-off about the possibility of the theft than I am and says he will get right back to me. I am thinking, *yeah, right...* Within minutes he calls me back. Turns out that in order to fix my truck, the technician had to go through the glove box. The technician who fixed my truck thought the ear phones might have fallen out of the glove box so he them put back in the glove box. Doh! My bad.

The service manager then called me back, but he had no idea what had occurred. I could tell he thought this was going to be another angry-customer call. I told him that this was originally going to be a complaint call, but now it was a call to tell him what a great job the service advisor did—that he called me right back, promptly dealt with the problem and even had my truck ready when he said it would be. In short, he did a great job and I thought the manager should know. Can you guess what his initial response was? "Wow, thank you. I never get calls like this…" If you want to make somebody's day, tell them they did a good job after they waited on you. It is amazing to watch how unprepared they are for a compliment.

The easiest way to provide great customer service is to understand your customer. Learn to speak their language and meet their expectations. For instance, what income bracket are they from? You sell to affluent customers differently than low-income customers. Listen to a radio or TV advertisement for a car dealership. If the car on sale is a low-price model, the announcer is screaming: ACT NOW! ACT NOW! THESE PRICES ARE SO LOW; THEY ARE INSANE! ONLY $2.00 A MONTH FOR THE NEXT FORTY YEARS AND THIS CAR IS YOURS! Now watch an ad for a luxury car – no screaming going on there.

Are your customers only concerned about price? Or is quality as important? How about image? Learn to understand what their expectations are of you and your products before you try to sell to them.

Finally, treat your customers with respect; say, "Thank you," and make them feel special. No matter how pissed-off they make you. Remember, the bar is set really low…

Sales Reps

Here are a few more things about sales reps that will help you get better results out of your sales team.

1. Give them a quota. Every rep needs to be measured against a number. Just giving a rep a quota will increase his or her production by ten percent.

2. Pay a commission. A sales rep that works for salary only is not a sales rep.

3. Reps should pay for themselves. If they are not covering their cost with overhead and a profit, get rid of them.

4. Managing a sales rep is very different than managing other employees. The term "herding cats" comes to mind. You cannot manage a sales team the same way you manage administration or operations. Try that, and the sales team will fail every time.

Marketing

What works? To be honest, I don't think anybody really knows anymore. I belong to a small gym that markets to a fixed geographic territory. Most every time I am there (three times a week), I see staff stuffing flyers into plastic bags. They drop these flyers in people's driveways as a form of marketing. Being a business consultant, I was naturally curious as to what kind of response they get with this marketing effort. The owner told me that if they drop five-thousand driveway flyers, they will get about fifty responses – about a .01 percent response rate. He also said that if they do a ten-thousand-piece direct-mail campaign, they will get twenty-five responses – about a .0025 percent response rate. I asked him what they get off of the Internet and he bluntly said, "Not a thing." Interesting, a driveway drop beats the Internet... I have not seen that in any marketing books lately.

Let's take an honest look at several types of marketing for small businesses:

Networking

For the sake of full disclosure, I admit that I don't like to attend networking events or leads groups. I don't have the patience for the inane banter that tries to masquerade as conversation. I love speaking at the groups, but I do not like being a participant. *BUT THIS IS JUST ME.* A lot of people LOVE these types of events and get great value out of them. If you do not like to attend these meetings, just be honest about it. It is very hard to fake it, so try something else.

There is no shortage of networking opportunities for business owners who want to get out there and meet people. There are leads groups, Chamber of Commerce networking meetings, business associations, the Rotary Club, Kiwanis International – you name it, and you can find it. The pros and cons of these types of meetings are many. But ultimately it comes down to whether you like to attend these meetings and if your type of business can benefit from your participation.

A former client of mine owned an accounting firm. They decided they needed to send their accountants to networking meetings to help drive new business. I happened to be at a networking event (my wife asked me to go with her...) prior to picking them up as a client. I noticed a couple of their accountants huddled in a corner together nursing a drink.

They were not networking, and it was very obvious to anybody who paid any attention that they did not want to be there. In fact, if you had given them the choice of attending the networking meeting or having a root canal, they would have chosen the root canal. So their very attendance was actually a detriment to the firm.

When I pointed this out to the owner, his first response was that he was going "to make them start networking the right way." I had to point out that they are ACCOUNTANTS, not salespeople. You are asking them to commit unnatural acts. No matter how hard he was going to try, they were not going to change their basic behavior. Why? Because they hated networking.

On another occasion, I was speaking to a networking group and arrived a few minutes early. I was networking with the audience to get a feel for the types of people in the room and what they hoped to get out of the presentation. A young woman came up to me to introduce herself and her business. At the time she did not know I was the speaker, so she must have thought I was a potential prospect. She was clearly not comfortable in this networking environment and she seemed to be over-compensating for something. I remember thinking that I admired her grit for doing something that she clearly was uncomfortable doing but she was trying anyway. At one point in this very awkward conversation, she mentioned something about her baby. Note that this was completely out of context with anything we were discussing. So trying to be polite, and assuming she wanted to talk about children, I asked how old her baby was. She whipped out the keys to her BMW and dangled them in my face, saying that this was her baby. My admiration went to pity as I wondered what possessed her to want to impress me with the knowledge that she drove a BMW. She just ended up looking like some idiot that I would never consider doing business with. I seriously doubt that was her intention when she left the house that morning: "I think I will go to a networking meeting this morning and make a complete ass of myself…" Are you one of these people at these meetings trying way too hard to impress people?

In order for networking to work for you, you have to remember one very important rule: Do not go to a networking meeting expecting to sell something. Nobody ever got up in the morning with back pain and said, "Boy, my back hurts, I think I'll go to the chamber meeting today and find a chiropractor." Or Aunt Mable leaves you some inheritance money: do you go to a networking meeting to find a financial planner? No. Nobody is there looking to buy your product or service, either. What makes networking work is when you help other people in attendance find business. This helps build trust and relationships, which ultimately is what it is all about. It also takes a long time. Successful networking is a long-term strategy. You can't just show up every couple of months and expect it to work.

A note about leads groups: each group has its own personality and rules. I was a guest at a meeting where the first ten minutes was spent debating the difference between a lead and a prospect. Seems it was important because they track the number of leads one member gives to other members. The solution was to have the attorney in the group meet with people afterwards to reach some resolution. Oh, great, let's get the attorney involved... Turns out that if you did not pass along enough leads to other members, you were out of the group. If you missed too many meetings, you were out of the group. If you were late, you were fined a dollar. Too many fricking rules, so I was out...

Bottom line is I am not a "group" kind of guy so these types of meetings are not the best use of my time. It also saves me attorney's fees because I don't have to worry about clocking some idiot who wants to fine me a dollar.

Online Social Networking

Somebody finally figured out how to take a complete waste of time, wrap it in a pretty dress, say it is marketing, and now have the excuse to be on Facebook all day at work. "I am networking!" People frequently ask me, "Are you on Facebook?" My answer right now is no because, if I am going to waste time in cyberspace, it will be on my Xbox 360, killing mutants in some post-apocalyptic world. I always get the same response: "Oh, but you should; it is awesome!" To which I respond, "But have you gotten any business from it?" The answer is usually along the lines of: "No, but you would not believe the friends from high school who have found me!" The wife of one of my clients made a salient point about Facebook and all of these long-lost "friends." Maybe these friendships died for a reason... And let's not even talk about ex-lovers... What possible good can come from that?

Another thing I don't get about Facebook is letting people know what you are doing at any given moment. I don't care what you are thinking, where you are about to go, or that you are folding your clothes. And I totally don't get stalking applications like Twitter. If I want you to know where I am, I will let you know. Call me weird, call me antisocial, but just don't Twitter me...

Direct Mail and Email Campaigns

If you have been in business, you have done (or thought about doing) a direct-mail campaign. A lot of work and money goes into one of these campaigns. First, you have to have a good list of names. There are numerous websites where you can get a list of names that match the criteria of your prospects. You need to understand a couple of things about these lists; first, ten to fifteen percent of the names will be bad. I suspect in this current economy, that number is going to be higher. And second, people lie about their company information. It is amazing how many businesses that list they have two to five employees are actually single proprietors. They lie because they do not want to look small.

Then there are the costs for printing, postage, paper, ink, envelopes, and labor. It can get quite expensive. What do you think the average response rate for a direct-mail campaign from a cold list is? If you get .0025 percent, you are doing great. That is not twenty-five percent. It is one quarter of one percent. This is not customers; it is responses. Depending on your close rate, this number gets *really* small. If you have the wrong message and are attracting the wrong prospect, your costs go up even higher as you have to chase and service inquiries from prospects that are never going to buy in the first place. Ouch.

Finally, ask yourself this question. When you receive a direct-mail letter or flyer, do you actually read it? Probably not. The same thing happens to your direct-mail letters.

The same can be said for email. How many email campaigns actually even make it to you? Chances are your email winds up in somebody's junk-mail box, right next to the scams from Nigeria and the Viagra emails.

Bottom line for both email and direct-mail campaigns; it is a numbers game. A huge numbers game that most business owners wind up losing. You need to have the right list that matches your prospect profile and has up-to-date information. Your messaging needs to be spot-on. If you happen to get lucky and your piece gets into the hands of the intended target, you have about a millisecond to grab their attention. If you don't, the reader does not get past the headline before your very pretty, expensive piece of mail winds up in the garbage. And, oh yeah, make sure it is not against the law in your state. Other than that, go for it. Kind of like hunting for mosquitoes with a BB gun.

Cold Calling

When was the last time you took a cold call from a sales rep who you did not know? Yeah, I know, your cold call will be different. Again, this has become a huge numbers game with a very small hit rate. That does not mean it does not work. Hell, the Nigerians still get people sending them their bank account information from spam emails. The question becomes do you use an in-house telemarketer or hire an outside firm? I can argue both sides of the coin. Hiring and managing in-house telemarketers is a royal pain in the ass with high turnover. You will be constantly looking for new employees and redefining micromanagement. On the other hand, an outside firm can be a crap shoot as well. I once hired a telemarketing firm to find leads from a very specific list of names from a very specific industry. One day, one of my reps comes to me with a lead from the telemarketing company and asked me if they should pursue it because our software was not designed for this industry. It turns out that the lead was not even from our list, let alone our industry. So I called the telemarketing company to ask them why we even got the lead and to make sure they were not charging us. Amazingly, they did not seem to understand that I had a problem with the lead. IT WAS A LEAD! The telemarketer was so excited about the lead that he could not even understand that I would not want it. IT WAS A LEAD! About a month later they went out of business. Back in the nineties, I knew of a telemarketing firm that had female prison inmates make their calls.

Yellow Pages

The only time I go to the Yellow Pages is to find a plumber and that is probably out of habit and usually because I need somebody right away. Certain businesses seem to be a better fit for the Yellow Pages than others. Ask yourself this question: when was the last time you used the Yellow Pages? If you are like most people, it was sometime last year. I don't think my twenty-year-old daughter even knows what the Yellow Pages are.

Online Ads

The science of online ads is very sophisticated. I am starting to notice that all of a sudden, a lot of the pop-up ads I see are from companies selling soccer equipment. Is this because I did an on-line search for soccer equipment? Or is it because I purchased soccer equipment from an online company? Either way, it seems rather Orwellian to me, and I don't like it. Hire a professional to help you with online messaging and placement. It has become too complicated for mere mortals.

Websites

What is the purpose of your site? It is an online brochure or a retail site? Does it really matter what your web-page ranking is when somebody does a search on the Internet for your company or product? For some businesses it is vitally important. For other businesses it is not. Again, if you are like most people, hire a professional to help you with search engine optimization. It can be a full-time job just trying to keep your site on the first page of a search.

If you have a tight budget, there are some very inexpensive website providers that provide standard templates from which to create your site. The messaging as well as the look and feel is very important. An ugly site will drive away customers. A slow site will drive away customers. If you are not good at graphic design and messaging, hire a professional to help with your site. Don't kid yourself, a half-assed site looks like a half-assed site.

Newspaper Ads

The newspaper business is going out of business. This is partly because of demographics and partly because of content. For older guys like me, I like reading the paper on Sunday mornings. But my daughter gets all of her information online. Another reason is that with the Internet and cable news, combined with a 24/7 news cycle, chances are I have already heard or read about an event before I even pick up the morning paper so it is no longer news.

On New Year's Day, I was featured on the front page of the business section of the largest local newspaper in Atlanta. Shortly after that, I was speaking to a group of more than one hundred people and I asked the audience how many had seen the article. Not a single person raised their hand!

The next time you read a paper, I want you to notice the number of ads you actually read. We have developed this ability to not even see ads unless we happen to be in the market for a particular product or service. If you do decide to run an ad, you have to run it many times to get a response. No, the ad rep is not lying to you when they say you need to buy a series of ads. Your headline and messaging is also very important for the reasons listed earlier. Don't do what most people do and use their company name as the headline. Nobody cares.

Hope is not a strategy.

I once heard a story about a business owner on a marketing panel who said that his marketing strategy was HOPE. He HOPED the phone would ring. This was never was a good strategy in the first place, but given the changes in the economic climate it is now business suicide.

So what the hell works? GREAT QUESTION! If somebody tells you they have the answer, they are lying. If you are a small business, getting leads is going to be one of the hardest tasks you have to manage. Small business owners typically cannot afford big expensive direct-mail or telemarketing campaigns. So focus on word-of-mouth referrals, and alliances. They are your best sources of leads. Focus there first. Second, find some outside help. Check with peers in your industry about what works for them. If they tell you they get a certain number of responses from a certain type of campaign, ask to see the numbers. Chances are they do not track them and they are giving you a gut reaction anyway.

The bottom line for most small business owners is to hire a professional. One who can help put together the messaging and the proper campaigns for a business. If you do not have a sales background, do not attempt this or you will just be wasting money. Most people complain about their results when they try a marketing campaign. That is because they usually do it wrong. The messaging is designed by a brother-in-law and the website is designed by a cousin. Hey, at least it was cheap...

SECTION IV

EMPLOYEES

CHAPTER 24

EMPLOYEES ARE A PAIN IN THE @$$...

Two things are infinite: the universe and human stupidity;
and I'm not sure about the universe.
~ Albert Einstein

Of all the sections in this book that has the potential to piss off somebody or offend the sensitivities of the "politically correct," this one leads the pack. If you are from HR or a kumbaya type, then skip this section. Otherwise, sit back and enjoy the ride.

When we were in the process of buying a franchise, one of the companies we looked at was a maid franchise. The main reason we did not buy this franchise was that we realized it would be nothing but a huge human resource problem combined with language issues. Since I was not particularly interested in learning another language so I could speak with my employees, and I did not want the hassle of dealing with a large number of hourly workers, we purchased a coaching franchise which did not require employees. Why? Employees are a pain in the @$$.

Employees will never care as much as you do. They are your greatest asset and your biggest liability, usually a combination of both. Either way, they are still a pain in the @$$. The most likely person to sue you is an existing or ex-employee. They call in sick and bring their personal problems to work. They lie, cheat, and steal. If you are lucky, this is the worst they will do. Harsh? Nope, ask any business owner who is not trying to be politically correct and they will wholeheartedly agree.

Part of the politically correct movement has created a culture where people think it is the responsibility of the business owner to take care of the employees when they bring personal issues into the workplace. It is not your responsibility to babysit your employees or be their rescue net. It is your responsibility to provide your employees with the tools required to do their job in a positive work environment. It is your responsibility to make sound business decisions that help the company grow. Keeping a problem employee on board is usually not a sound business decision. These employees cost you customers, productivity, revenue, morale, and potential lawsuits.

When the business owner starts making exceptions for underperforming employees, the whole organization suffers and the good employees start lowering their performance to the lowest common denominator. Make exceptions for one, and you have to make exceptions for *EVERYBODY*.

One example I see a lot is letting an employee work from home because they are a "disruption" to the office. You know the kind – no social skills and should be locked in a room and fed under the door. I had one business owner tell me that letting one of his problem employees work from home was not an issue because the rest of the employees knew that this was not a reward. I had to respectfully disagree. If I am one of the other employees, I am going to start being a disruption because now I don't have a commute, I save gas money, and I can watch the *Jerry Springer Show* from the comfort of my own bed. My solution was to convert the employee to a contractor and use him on an as-needed basis. Now he is no longer a disruptive employee working from home; he is a contractor working less hours from home.

Employees are the number-one component of your business that will make or break your company. There is a reason factories are going fully robotic. Robots don't go on strike, shoot each other, or try to burn down the business when they get pissed off. Robots don't call in sick, do drugs, or engage in petty politics. They just work. The really good ones even tell you when they are about to breakdown. This beats getting the call on the last day of the month that Sue can't come in because she's under the weather (partied too hard last night).

I know of a business that had an employee burn down part of their building because she "thought" she was going to get fired. Imagine her surprise when she learned that prior to the act of arson she was not the one getting fired. It was somebody else in the organization. Rumor mills can be brutal.

There is no shortage of books or advice about employees and how to build the perfect team. But they all seem to miss that one very important fact – employees are *a pain in the ass*. I know there may be HR professionals having seizures because of my "insensitivity." Get over it. Ask any small business owner what is their biggest headache and almost universally you will hear: Cash flow is number one and employees are number two. As the business gets bigger, these two will tend to switch in order of importance.

Whenever I hear this drivel that "all people are created equal," I have to laugh. The simple truth is that some people are more equal than others. Why is it that people are willing to agree that some athletes are better than others, yet are reluctant to admit that some people are smarter than others? It is because of political correctness and its sibling "Let's not judge anybody." The truth is, there are stupid people, smart people, and everything in between. One of the goals of a business owner should be to *not* hire the stupid people and everything in between. Employees will make or break your company – period. Hire the best and do not hire anybody without putting them through a real hiring process and requiring the candidate to take a behavioral assessment.

If you are fortunate to find one of the good ones, do everything you can to keep them. Make the other employees live up to their standards, not the other way around. The good ones are worth their weight in gold.

CHAPTER 25

YOU CAN'T FIX YOUR EMPLOYEES "ISSUES"...

No. no, of course not. We find it's always better to fire people on a Friday.
Studies have statistically shown that there's less chance of an incident
if you do it at the end of the week.
~ Office Space, 1999

It amazes me that people will be maniacally paranoid about who they let into their homes but will hire an employee without anything other than a gut feeling that "they seem nice." Beware of the "nice guy."

A 1999 Slate.com article, "What's Wrong With the Neighbors?" by Hanna Rosin and David Plotz, had the following quotes:

> "I thought he was pretty nice ... but then again, I knew that his beliefs were way out of line. They were good neighbors, but, well, I got blue eyes, so I guess that helps."
> — *Meda VanDyke on her neighbor, neo-Nazi murderer Buford Furrow*

> "He used to say, 'They're watching me, through your satellite dish.' I'd tell him, 'No, no, Rusty, no, they aren't watching you.' I tried to convince him, but it made no difference ... He was just a regular guy when he didn't have this problem. Everybody said, 'He's harmless.'"
> — *Ken Moore, on his neighbor, U.S. Capitol murderer Russell Weston*

"We figured they would have questioned him and let him go
and eventually we forgot about it."
— *Eric Anderson, neighbor of Atlanta mass murderer Mark Barton,
on the murder of Barton's first wife and mother-in-law several
years earlier*

Jeffrey Dahmer's neighbors, for example, told reporters: "He was
shy, a little withdrawn. But not real bizarre," and that, "he never bothered
anyone." (Anyone? What about all those people he ate?)

According to his neighbors, Columbine killer Eric Harris was "a
nice guy. Shy person, didn't say much" and "a very nice, polite, clean-cut
kid." Furrow's neighbors called him, "a very pleasant individual." Barton's
neighbors saw him as "a typical American family man, a nice guy" who
"kept to himself."

It is always the "quiet guy" who seemed "nice" that goes on a
killing spree.

Hiring the right person is one of the single most important
activities you will do as a business owner. Yet, amazingly it is one of the
least thought about things most business owners will do. As one client
said to me, "My hiring process used to be: Hey you showed up for the
interview; you seem nice, when can you start?"

I am not saying that everybody you hire has the potential to be a
serial murderer or go postal, uh, never mind, yes I am saying that…

Why are employees a pain in the ass? The answers are many
and all are frustrating. One of the root causes is that entrepreneurs and
employees are fundamentally wired differently. Just like men and women.
I can't count the number of times a business owner has expressed total
frustration and confusion over an employee's behavior. Not a week goes
by that I am not dealing with a client's employee issue.

One of my favorite complaints that I hear from business owners
is: "Why can't my employees leave their personal problems at home?" Do
you? Of course not, nobody does. Simply put, it is impossible. We live in
a "reality show" society of victims with an entitlement attitude that knows
no bounds. What a frightening combination.

Larger companies can absorb the damage of a dysfunctional
employee. Corporations will help rehabilitate an employee because they
will wind up with "a better employee." Yeah right. I am sure that happens

sometimes, but not typically. It just makes the kumbaya-types in the HR department feel good. The primary motivation of the company is not to be sued because of the Americans with Disabilities Act of 1990. And a little good PR never hurt anybody… It is getting to a point where almost any issue can fall under the act. I am trying to figure out how I can get "saying what I think" to fall under the act. After all, it has caused me to get fired on several occasions, and isn't that what it is all about?

Somewhere near the other side of the coin is the "not quite bad enough" employee. We all have them, the employee that just skates along, doing the absolute minimum amount of work so that they don't draw attention. They know there is ALWAYS somebody worse than them and they don't care who is better.

You know they aren't doing their best or pulling their weight but there always seems to be other employees causing bigger problems so you never get around to doing anything about it. Every time they get back on your radar, another problem pops up. Then one day you look up and they have been with your company for years.

The problem with these employees (beyond the obvious) is that they lower the performance of the entire staff. EVERYBODY knows what this person gets away with and how they never seem to be held accountable. Human nature being what it is, people start lowering their standards to the bar of the "not quite bad enough" employee.

Don't fall victim to this scourge.

CHAPTER 26

YOU CANNOT AFFORD DRUGS AND ALCOHOL IN YOUR BUSINESS...

Alcoholism is the only disease that you can get yelled at for having.
~ Mitch Hedberg

This section is very close to my heart and I know of what I speak from personal experience. This is going to be one of the more "cold-hearted" sections of the book. I am not an alcoholic but my family tree is riddled with this affliction, including both of my parents. My attitude is seasoned from years of manipulation and lies from those around me with both drug and alcohol problems. My father was sober the last ten years of his life. He had to go to A.A. meetings every day as he struggled to maintain his sobriety. I still tear up at the memory of me giving him his first year of sobriety chit. When he died he was my best friend.

It took getting his third DUI and having to spend the weekend in jail, losing his license to drive for five years, and house arrest for a year to get him to sober up. Now – do you really think as an employer you have the ability and power to get an alcoholic to change? No, you do not.

The reality is rehab fails more often than it works. My simple advice is this: If you suspect an employee has a drug problem, fire them. The sooner the better. The odds are they are not going to "get better" or "see the error of their ways." I have a client who tried to help an employee with a drug problem. Their reward was being lied to, more excuses, higher absenteeism, and money stolen from petty cash. They were just shocked she would do that to them. After all, "she had worked there for four years!"

My response was, "Why? She is lying and cheating on everybody around her. What makes you so special?"

I was the VP and general manager of a small flooring company and we had a group of about twenty-five laborers. I had one employee who was living out of his car and was just recently off drugs (so he said). He started making more money than he had made in his entire life. He was getting ready to move into an apartment and turn his life around. I was "the man" to him and I felt very proud about my part in his turnaround. One weekend, he failed to show up for work. I finally got another employee to tell me what had happened. It seems he decided his new-found wealth was better spent on crack than an apartment. I fired him. No discussion, no excuses, no debate. I could not afford it and I did not have the time to try and "fix" him. Not my job.

Somewhere somebody is screaming, "This is not true! Look what happened to Betty when we helped her! She turned it around!" Yes, there are exceptions to everything. But to me this is like playing one of ten-thousand slot machines and winning, and then claiming they are all going to win just because you play them. You can only help somebody with a drug or alcohol problem when *that person* is ready to be helped. Unfortunately, this is usually when the person has crashed and burned and has no other choice.

If you are a small business, you cannot afford to rehabilitate alcohol or drug-addicted employees. Do you know what the average rehabilitation rate for crystal meth is? Less than five percent! Run, Forrest, run, run like hell…

CHAPTER 27

THE INTERNET WASTES JUST AS MUCH TIME
AS IT SAVES (PROBABLY MORE)...

*There's a statistical theory that if you gave a million monkeys typewriters
and set them to work, they'd eventually come up with the complete works of
Shakespeare. Thanks to the Internet, we know this isn't true.*
~ Ian Hart

We have all heard it; productivity soars because of the Internet! Not sure I believe it. I have seen statistics that say that the average employee spends forty-four percent or more of their day on the Internet. Forty-four percent or higher! For women, it is shopping, chat rooms, and instant messaging. For men, the top-three types of sites are porn, sports, and gambling. The hours of eight A.M. to five P.M. are the busiest times for porn-site traffic. I guess Internet access is faster at work and the wife is not looking over their shoulder. A productivity enhancer may be buying all of your male employees DSL Internet access at home and going dial-up at the office. I hear it takes a long time to download porn on a dial-up connection...

Bottom line is that you need to block access to these sites. There are plenty of products that will help you do this. On top of the lost productivity issue, there are also liability issues. You can be sued for sexual harassment because an employee had porn on their system and you did nothing about. The FBI can seize all of your computers if you have an employee downloading kiddie porn – even if you were not aware of it. Is it really worth the risk? If you want to see how bad this problem really is, or if you need help, read *Porn at Work* by Michael Leahy. The problem is huge and underreported.

CHAPTER 28

MARRIAGE AND DIVORCE PROBLEMS
DO NOT STAY AT HOME...

Lady Nancy Astor: *Winston, if you were my husband, I'd poison your tea.*
Winston Churchill: *Nancy, if I were your husband, I'd drink it.*

Supposedly, fifty percent of marriages fail. So that begs the question; if fifty percent fail, what percentage of the other fifty percent really suck but they don't do anything about it? Twenty-five percent? Forty percent? A more cynical person might say that seventy-five percent of your married employees do not have it very good at home. And that fun at home does follow them to the office.

I have seen my own employees crash and burn because of a divorce. I have seen my client's employees do the same. Chances are they will not be hitting on all cylinders during the divorce, so there goes productivity. I am not necessarily advocating replacing this person but you do need to be extra vigilant. Depending on the person, it can also lead to drug and alcohol problems. Chances are it is going to be an ugly ride for a while – usually a year or two.

This leads to one of the consequences of divorce – single parents. And this situation almost always falls on the mother. One of the best employees I ever had was a single mother. Although she was one of my best employees, I had to make exceptions based on her family situation. Kids get sick, injured, or any one of a million things that can go wrong. It is unrealistic to expect that a single parent will be able to keep family circumstances separate from work. Just know that when you hire a single parent, you get the WHOLE package.

Don't expect anything less.

Everybody has personal issues. Some just handle them better than others. I believe it has to do with how we were raised and how we are wired – the old nature vs. nurture debate. I know an owner of a hair salon who feels there is nothing you can do to change hard-wired personal issues. You may get short-term behavioral changes, but people always go back to the old behavior, no matter the consequences.

Now let's combine an employee with a bad marriage, addiction to porn, and a boatload of personal issues, and you have hit the trifecta. Problem is, this type of person is far more prevalent than you and I want to believe. And this combination directly affects the bottom line of your business. If you think that as an employer you can change the behavior of others with kindness, more money, or with "another chance," the odds are you are dead wrong. Unfortunately, small business cannot absorb the costs associated with some of the more popular dysfunctions and personal issues. Lost productivity, absenteeism, and higher insurance rates can all cripple a small business.

CHAPTER 29

YOU CANNOT COMPETE IF YOU ARE PLAYING
WITH A MINOR LEAGUE TEAM...

*The first method for estimating the intelligence of a ruler
is to look at the men he has around him.*
~ Niccolò Machiavelli 1469-1527

I live in the suburbs of Atlanta in Gwinnett County. We have an ECHL minor league hockey team called the Gwinnett Gladiators. Up until a couple of years ago, I was not a hockey fan. Under duress, we went to a Cub Scouts night at a Gladiator game. I was not expecting much since I was not a fan of hockey, let alone minor-league hockey. Much to my surprise, about halfway through the first period, I realized I was enjoying myself and cheering for a team I did not care about one hour ago.

We started going to more games and I began to understand the finer points of the sport, like the fights. Up until this point, our family's only exposure to hockey was two levels below the pros. My son caught the hockey bug and started watching the National Hockey League. He is now a huge fan of the Pittsburgh Penguins. I started watching NHL hockey and was absolutely amazed at the difference in the game that I was used to watching. NHL is much faster and the hits are much harder. In minor league hockey we are excited when a player makes a successful pass as this is the exception. In the NHL, a missed pass is the exception.

So why mention this in a business book, you ask? A couple of years ago, one of my clients was a reseller for a single software company. They sold software and services at price points averaging about $10K to $15K.

Because of market changes and a variety of other issues, we determined they needed to sell another product and be less dependent on the original software provider, so they picked up another product to resell.

Now their average deal size of software and services is $250K to $500K. That was the good news. The bad news was that when they first started implementing these large deals, the implementations started to blow up. They eventually were able to get these companies implemented, but it took a lot longer and cost a lot more money than had been estimated. There was much anxiety and gnashing of teeth as to why this was happening. It became clear that they needed a senior project manager with the skills to manage a big software implementation. The owner had the opportunity to hire a senior consultant with the exact skill set needed. As he said to me, "Kevin, this is either going to be the smartest move I have ever made or the dumbest. He is now going to be the highest-paid employee." It was amazing to watch this professional in action – he played at a different level. Suddenly, the rest of the employees were now being measured by a bar that had never been set that high.

They were now in the major leagues of software but were playing with a minor league team. The entire company had to be looked at from top to bottom. Whose skill sets could be upgraded? Who could make the transition? Who needed to be let go? These were the questions now being asked. The reality was they had successfully negotiated a new business strategy, but it was now the employees that were holding them back.

CHAPTER 30

DON'T HIRE FRIENDS AND FAMILY...

I'm a parent. I haven't got the luxury of principles.
~ Benjamin Martin in *The Patriot*, 2000

I have one piece of advice if you are thinking about working with friends or family – DON'T. Working with family and friends rarely turns out well. I have seen countless businesses flounder, struggle, or fail because of mixing family and business.

Friends...
Let's start with friends. No problem right? Just be prepared to have to fire them someday. For reasons I have not been able to understand, they seem to have this sense of entitlement that increases over time. I have seen it get to the point that the friend just "assumed" he would get part of the business. Go ahead and hire a friend, just as long as you don't care that the odds are in favor of losing the friendship in the not-too-distant future.

Spouses...
I have to be careful here since I work with my wife, Barbara. Just kidding... I am very fortunate to have an awesome wife. We understand each other's strengths and weaknesses. I am the consultant and public speaker and she is the operations/logistics person. Although we do confer with each other, we are very confident in each other's ability to handle

our roles so we do not tell each other how to do our jobs. Unfortunately, based on my experience with husband and wife teams, we are very much the exception. Most couples do not have these boundaries and there are constant struggles about how to do a task or when the task needs to be completed. Now take the normal discourse of business and throw in the emotional dynamic of a marriage. BOOM! Just like putting gasoline on the fire and, most of the time, it does not turn out well.

Human nature is a funny thing, opposites do attract. How often do you see a couple where the spouses are opposites? Most of the time. In order for the marriage/work thing to work smoothly, these differences have to be looked at as complementary skill sets instead of points of contention. Using the DiSC profile, I am a high double D and my wife is an S and C. If you are not familiar with DiSC, suffice it to say we are the epitome of opposites. We have very complementary skill sets but it does cause problems. For example, my wife would like to sit down every week and discuss what we are doing and make plans for the upcoming week. I have to admit that I am not very good at having this meeting. Why? Because I don't think it is necessary. So who is right and who is wrong? Neither; it is just how we are wired. I should do the meetings more than I do. Why? Because communication is very important, especially in a marriage. Also, because it makes my wife happy. I am still working on trying to be better at this endeavor. *Trying* being the operative word.

As I said before, I am very lucky to have a great wife. She doesn't scream and yell or nag me about the lack of meetings, but she does get frustrated. That is not the case with a lot of the husband-and-wife teams I have worked with in the past. I have seen business issues wreck many a marriage. My opinion is that it is because there are no longer any boundaries between home and work. It is now just one big battlefield. There is no place to recharge because the battle follows you home and right into bed. Despite what some of the PC minions say, men and women are different. We view things differently, we think differently, we speak differently. As a general rule, men are much better than women at leaving work at the office. A man thinks he can have a fight with his wife at work during the day and then go home have sex with her that night. Even when the fight was worked out before they went home, the odds are not that great…

The downward spiral is sometimes fast and sometimes slow. One spouse starts losing respect for the other. The very personality traits that attracted each to the other in the first place become the primary bones of contention. She is a control freak and wants too much detail… He is too aggressive and does not listen…

My experience is that husband-and-wife teams are a delicate balancing act. Most of the time, we wind up losing our balance. I have heard stories about spouses divorcing but staying in the business together. I know a sales rep who lasted one day at a new job because of these very circumstances. During the interview process, everything seemed fine. First day on the job, a fellow employee pulled him aside and said he needed to leave, and leave now, because the working conditions were so bad due to constant fighting of the divorced owners. It sounded like this guy was being held prisoner. Not sure why he didn't leave. About halfway through the day, the sales rep met the owners at the copier and asked for clarification on a task. A simple question turned into huge fight between the owners – a verbal barrage that included the dreaded "C" word. He resigned right there. Talk about world war three…

Bottom line is this: no business is worth a marriage. If your marriage is suffering because of your business, one of you needs to get out. Do it before there is too much damage to the marriage. It is just not worth it.

Siblings…

My only real problem with nepotism is that I never had the chance to inherit a business. It just burns me up when I see a parent attempt to pass down a business to an ungrateful son or daughter who does not appreciate the opportunity they are being given.

On the other hand, I see business owners who want to create a legacy for their children and leave them the business but they are blind to some very important facts. The parents tend to still see their offspring as "children" and because of that they make a very common mistake: over-estimating their children's abilities. Nobody likes to look at their offspring and realize they may not be the brightest bulbs in the pack and they are not capable of running a business. Sports skills are a good example. While coaching my son's soccer team, I am both amused and saddened to see parents who think their "little Johnny" is an all-star, when in reality Johnny is one of the worst players on the field. Just as sad, is that ALL of the other employees in such a business are keenly aware of the offspring's limitations. The owner always seems to be the last to know.

I worked with a retail business that was owned by a husband and wife. Each had an adult child from a previous marriage, who was working there. The plan when they bought the store was to grow the business and then leave it to the two siblings to run and the parents would collect an annuity from the business. That was to be their retirement income.

On the first day I worked with them, I interviewed both of the siblings. It was apparent early in the conversation that neither was capable of running the business. In fact, one should not even have been working there. After the interviews, I told the owners that it was "time for plan B." They asked, "What was plan A?" My response was "Having your kids run this business. I see nothing to indicate that either one of them has the required skill set. In fact, one needs to be out of here and the other is just a good employee. Nothing more." They looked at me with pained expressions and finally said, "You are probably right." They garnered the courage to talk to the one that needed to be out of there and started helping him find another job.

This was a huge step for this family, but it often takes somebody from the outside to point out the obvious. The reality is that both parents knew what I was telling them – I just confirmed what they both knew in their gut. If you have your adult children working for you, what is your gut telling you?

In almost all cases where there are more than one sibling involved, one of the children is much more capable of running the business than the other(s). Result? Instant sibling rivalry. "Dad is playing favorites; that is not fair," or "Mom always liked you better." You may not hear it, but it is happening.

Another problem is that the child may not want the business, but is afraid to say so. It is amazing how often nobody talks about the situation and just goes through life with the wrong set of assumptions. Make sure you have an open and honest conversation with your children if you have plans for leaving the business to them. You will probably be surprised by what you hear.

I read a sobering statistic about family-run businesses and how there are not very good odds upon which to bank your retirement.

- Thirty percent of businesses survive the second generation – three of ten.

- Thirty percent of those businesses survive the third generation – one of ten.

Here is another painful example. I became involved with a business when the owner had quadruple-bypass surgery and was unable to run the business. He asked me to come on as VP and general manager to run the company. The goal was to grow the business and sell it. I would get forty percent and he would get sixty percent. Did I mention his three sons worked in the business, doing the labor? Minor detail…

I started towards the end of August, a month in which they had $19,000 in revenue and five employees. By December of that year, we had revenues of $180,000 for the month and more than twenty-five employees. The problem started when the owner suggested we implement a drug-testing program so we could obtain lower insurance rates. Great idea! I was then told by the office manager (office managers know everything) that all three sons were doing drugs. When I brought this up to the owner, he was in complete denial that this could even be possible – even though all of the sons had prior known problems with drugs. The owner's constant refrain was, "Oh, no, they are all clean, now!" So I started pushing for the drug tests and he suddenly was not interested anymore.

It came to a head when I started to get calls from our customers that our employees were sleeping on the job sites (including the sons). At the same time, we started having problems on all jobs the sons were involved with. I confronted the owner with an ultimatum – we start drug testing or I was out of there. His feeble response was, "Please don't make me choose you over my sons." By saying that, he had already made his choice. I left the company shortly thereafter because I could not overcome the powerful force of a father's denial. He went out of business nine months later, broke with no retirement – all because he would not see clearly and deal with his sons' drug problems.

Why wasn't the problem obvious earlier? When I first started, I had the laborers complaining to me that they needed to make more money or "My ol' lady is going to leave me." By December, they were making more money than they had made in a long time. For some, it was more money that they had ever made in their lives. Problem was, I was working them all of the time. Now the complaint was: "My ol' lady is going to leave me because I work too much." The other problem was they now had the money to buy drugs. Can't win for losing…

Fire your son-in-law

The problem with in-laws is that they seem to come in two forms. They think they know more than they actually do, or they are actually smarter than the family members. Both come with their own landmines.

I have counseled numerous business owners to fire an in-law. They knew they needed to do it but could not because of what I call "The fear of Thanksgiving dinner." They did not want to have face their daughter and tell her they have to fire her husband. They also did not want to have to deal with the subsequent fallout at the next Thanksgiving dinner when they had to sit across the table from both of them.

I know of a construction company that was started by a father out of the back of his pick-up truck. The business started to grow significantly when one of his sons joined the company. He was extremely bright and ambitious and was taking the business to the next level. The problem was the son-in-law who worked at the business. To put it in simple terms (the son's): "He is a dumb-ass and does not know it." In fact, the son-in-law felt he was responsible for all the changes and growth in the business. The son wanted the son-in-law fired and finally had to point blank tell the father it is "either him or me." The father hoped it would all go away and did nothing. The son left, the son-in-law is still there, and the business is treading water. All because the father did not want to have to face "the Thanksgiving dinner."

One of the main problems with friends, in-laws, and relatives of the business owner is that they often feel that the rules don't apply to them. Their sense of entitlement seems to get worse over the years and can become a cancer in the organization. If employees see a family member getting away with something they are not allowed to do, morale suffers. Understand that whether or not the friend or family member is actually receiving preferential treatment, the perception of the other employees is that they are.

Helicopter Parents

In the July 2008 edition of *O – The Oprah Magazine* (my wife reads it…), there is an article titled "Look! Up in the sky! It's a bird! It's a plane! It's…Supermom!" The teaser on the cover for the article is: "MOM DRIVES 2HRS TO DO SON'S LAUNDRY!" There is another teaser for an article titled: "WHY MEN DO STUPID THINGS" but that is a topic for another time…

The article was about "helicopter parents." Helicopter parents are the over-indulgent parents who put their darling Johnny at the center of the universe. Every scribble Johnny produces is a work of art and deserves to be on the refrigerator. As Johnny grows older, the role of the parent is to be at the beck and call of the chosen one. The number of children in their twenties and thirties still living at home is amazing and still growing – making it easier for these young people to coast along without making sacrifices or efforts on their own. This helps to create a world where there is no pain or discomfort for little Johnny. Unfortunately, that is not the real world.

The subtext of the article illuminated the impact these child-rearing practices are already having on the business world. According to the article, some parents are calling Fortune 500 companies on behalf of their children to discuss offer letters and benefits – or to discuss vacation time because "we take two weeks off as a family at Christmas." It is not unheard of for such parents to attend the job interview. This has gotten so bad that some companies are setting up conference calls with the parents of perspective employees or even proactively sending the parents copies of the offer letter and benefits package.

I have briefly entertained the thought of going back to corporate America just for the chance to have a parent show up at an interview. Man, would that be fun, short, but fun…

My personal opinion is that I do not have the patience to deal with a "little Johnny" who has always been at the center of the universe and now expects his employer to be just as fawning as his parents. These kids have an incredible sense of entitlement and studies have already shown that they have a high turnover rate as employees. If you can find a young person who does not exhibit these "entitlement tendencies," think seriously about hiring them. However, if they do – send them running for the door, but expect a call from their mother.

My daughter is a student at the University of Georgia. She has numerous friends in sororities. For those of you unfamiliar with the masochistic ritual of getting into a sorority, it is called "Rush." The freshman girls spend all day in the hot August Georgia sun pimping themselves at the different sorority houses in hopes of being asked to join. Mothers (helicopter parents) hide between the different houses in order to fix the hair of their daughters so they will look their best for the next group of sorority sisters. The fun part for the sorority sisters is that they get to judge which of the girls going through Rush is worthy of joining their little club. One of my daughter's friends told her that these were some of the criteria being used by these paragons of wisdom (AKA sorority sisters):

- One girl's parents did not buy her a new car so they must not have much money; therefore, she was not worthy enough to be in the sorority.
- Another girl had a *JOB* during the summer! OMG! She definitely was not up to standards.
- Another one looked like she was not wearing *real* pearls!

These girls are in for a rude awaking. If you are a helicopter parent, shame on you. I hope you have a fund set aside for therapy because, when your little precious gets into the real world, they are going to have quite a shock when they realize that nobody gives a $#!^.

Due to changing circumstances in corporate America, there are lots of unemployed, extremely qualified people with gray hair (some of it premature because of their experience in corporate America) who would be great assets to your company. Hire them first, unless it is a technology position. Unfortunately, these little brats kick our butts when it comes to technology.

CHAPTER 31

OKAY, MR. ATTILA THE HUN... NOW WHAT DO I DO?

I'm a people person, very personable. I absolutely insist on enjoying life.
Not so task-oriented. Not a work horse. If you're looking for a Clydesdale,
I'm probably not your man. Like, I don't live to work; it's more the other way
around. I work to live. Incidentally, what's your policy on Columbus Day?
~ Randy Dupree in *You, Me and Dupree* (2006)

L eadership

There is a saying that your business is a direct reflection of you. Another saying is that you get the employees you deserve. Both are true.

I have seen control-freak business owners subconsciously hire incompetent people just so they have the excuse to continue to try to do everything themselves. "They are going to do it wrong anyway; I might as well do it myself because I know it will be right..." Sound familiar? Be honest...

I once met with the owner of a company that had several large deals cancel within a couple of months due to the economy. The dollar loss represented almost twenty-five percent of the company's total revenue for the previous year. Needless to say, this was very painful and had a psychological impact on the business owner. How did this psychological damage manifest itself in the business? The place was a mess. Everywhere – including the owner's office. As I toured the facility, I was introduced to the G.M. His office was even worse. At least I think it was his office; I could not tell as it was such a mess. One of the covers on a fluorescent light in the ceiling was hanging loose. As I went through the warehouse, we went by a fenced-in area where they stored their electronic equipment. The sign on the cage door said: "This door is to remain locked at all times – NO EXCEPTIONS." The gate was wide open and there was nobody around.

The owner had checked out. When I brought this to their attention, they admitted they were no longer looking forward to coming into work and the place did not used to look this way. This was a prime example of how a business is a direct reflection of the owner. If your business is a mess, you attract people who don't mind working in a mess. This usually means they are not attentive to the details or just don't care. Or it could just mean they are slobs. Either way, you don't want them working for you. Customers don't like conducting business with a slob who does not care.

Rules and Expectations

Make sure your expectations of each employee are clearly established and written down. In the absence of rules, employees make up their own. If the inmates are running the asylum, it is your fault.

Hiring

Stop hiring the wrong people. I know this sounds simple, but you are the one who is responsible for the people who work for you. I had a client who was at her wits end because she "never" could find good employees. When I inquired about her hiring process, she said it went something like this:

"I meet them at Starbucks and if they show up, they are already halfway to being hired. If they don't look like serial murderers, they are a step closer. And if I like them after talking with them, I will make an offer."

Needless to say, hiring somebody because they showed up for the interview and you liked them rarely turns out well.

So… what to do? Have a hiring process. A hiring process includes the following:

- Conduct multiple interviews: Most people can fake their way through one interview. Most business owners don't like the process of interviewing. Because of this, they are hoping to like each candidate they interview so they can hurry up and get the process over with. If possible, the candidate's first and second interview should be with different people in the organization. Then interview the candidate yourself last. See what the person is like when they're tired and have used up their charm. It also saves you time because you are not having to interview all of the morons that show up looking for a job.

- Use behavioral assessments: There are many companies that offer these tests and they are worth every dime.
- Perform credit and background checks: Some object to this practice – something about invasion of privacy. B.S. Which would you rather have handling money in your company? Somebody with a high credit rating and little or no debt? Or somebody sitting on a huge chunk of credit card debt, a past bankruptcy, and a low credit score?
- Require drug testing: As I pointed out earlier in this section, drugs in the workplace is a bad thing. Nothing good comes from it. The best way to prevent having a drug problem in the workplace is to hire people who don't do drugs. Drug testing helps you in that endeavor. But be forewarned – you are going to lose some candidates that seem to be fine. When I was a VP of sales, the topic of drug testing came up in an executive meeting. The VP of development quickly replied that if we implemented drug testing, we would not have any programmers left. I suspect we might have lost some managers and executives as well. We never did implement that drug-testing program.

Firing

A major problem I have seen with the majority of business owners and managers is their inability to fire people. As an effective business owner/ manager, you have to learn to fire people quickly. We have all been guilty of this: "I can't fire Betty because the customers like her." Or how about, "I can't fire Mike because I will lose that deal." I have never regretted firing anybody. Never. None of the *I can'ts* ever happened.

Unless you have sadistic tendencies, nobody likes firing people.

It is rough on both parties and can be a very emotional experience if not controlled properly. Here are some ideas for helping a firing go "smoother."

Whenever possible, try to leave the person you are firing with at least a shred of dignity. There is no need to make a bad situation worse. Name calling or verbal abuse serves no purpose other than maybe getting your ass kicked in the parking lot.

Document all transgressions in writing and have the employee sign the document. If a firing comes as a complete surprise to the employee, you have probably not done your job as a manager. Employees want and need to know where they stand – so let them know. This includes the GOOD as well. Of course you can have documented the entire process and the employee may still act like they have no idea they are going to be fired.

I took over a sales team that had two underperforming sales reps. They were both way behind on their quotas. I put each one on a ninety-day plan that basically said they had to be at quota at the end of the ninety-day period or they were fired. At the end of the first thirty days, they were no closer to reaching their goal than they had been thirty days earlier but they were both convinced they could make it happen. At sixty days, they were in the same place and still convinced they were going to magically pull their sales numbers out of a hat and save their jobs. I basically told them that I did not believe there was any way they could make their numbers and I hoped that they were looking for another job.

After ninety days, D-day arrived. They had sold only a small percentage of what they needed to make their number so I called them into my office to let them go. The first rep was very gracious and thanked me for the opportunity. Later on, he even referred some business my way. The second rep? That did not go as well. He acted like this was the first time he had even heard that he might be fired for not hitting his number. He became angry and actually started debating me like that was going to change my mind. When this happens, you have to be very straight and to the point: "YOU ARE FIRED AND IT IS NOT UP FOR NEGOTIATION. CALM DOWN OR I AM CALLING SECURITY" *you complete dumbass.* I was just thinking the last part. I wanted to say it but I was not really interested in getting into a fight in the parking lot. Accordingly, if you are a female, it is advisable to have a male in the room to help an irate employee keep some perspective and also to serve as a witness. Sometimes you can't fix stupid.

Conversely, if you are a male firing a female, I highly recommend you have another person in the room (preferably another female). It would not be the first time a female was fired and then claimed sexual harassment. The story line usually goes something like: "Everything was fine until I was called into the boss' office and he made unwanted sexual advances towards me. When I said, "No," he threatened to fire me. When I told him, "No," again, he got angry and fired me." It then becomes a battle where the male boss has to prove he did not make the advances. A case of "he said/she said." Have a witness in the room and this will not happen (usually).

In conclusion, it is all about you and the type of person who is willing to work for you. There is always somebody who does not seem to mind working for a verbally abusive jerk. I did not get that gene so I don't understand it. If you are a verbally abusive jerk, you will find people to work for you. It does not make you right; it just makes them messed up.

Hire the right people and treat them with respect and dignity. You do not have to be their friend. In fact, it is my belief that you should avoid becoming too personal with your employees. It only makes it harder on the day you have to fire them.

If you luck out and hire any of the good employees – treat them very well. They are gold.

SECTION V

FINANCES

CHAPTER 32

DO THE MATH...

Remind people that profit is the difference between revenue and expense.
This makes you look smart.
~Scott Adams

This is a short but incredibly important section. It is not my goal to teach you accounting or how to become a bookkeeper. You do not need to understand debits and credits (although it greatly helps) to read a financial report. I am just trying to drive home the point that: whether or not you understand accounting, you *have* to understand what the numbers mean to effectively run your business.

There are four financial reports you need to understand: profit and loss, cash flow statement, accounts receivable aging, and the balance sheet. These reports will tell you where you are right now, and give you a projected look into the future. If you are just not wired to understand what they mean, hire competent counsel who can translate the information for you.

It still amazes me how many business owners do not have a clue about the numbers of their business. I met with a business owner recently that has been in business for over twenty years. He has not seen a P&L for a year but he knows he is losing money because the amount he owes on his credit line keeps growing. He sends his cash receipts and checks to the accountant, who then crunches the numbers to produce a P&L. Seems he is a little behind getting the accountant the latest information but the accountant is still charging him three hundred dollars a month for their bookkeeping services. I guess you get what you pay for.

I met with another business owner who was in the start-up mode. He had spent the last six months working on a business plan with some government organization offering free business consulting. After listening to him describe his business model, product, and pricing, I asked him how much he wanted to make a year. His immediate reply was, "At least 100K." The problem was that, based on his business plan, earning 100K was impossible. The numbers did not add up. It took me about two seconds to do the math and reach that conclusion. So I asked him if he had done the math. Of course, he had not. When I pulled out my calculator and showed him the bitter truth, he was visibly shaken. How can you spend six months building a business plan but never do the math? I guess free advice from a government organization is worth the price you pay for it...

Another example of not doing the math was a former client who made high-end cabinetry. When we first met, he was about to bring on his first manufacturers rep to sell his cabinets in another city. When I asked how he was going to pay the rep, he said something to the effect of: "Probably around ten percent. Does that sound about right?" When I asked, "Is that ten percent of gross sales or gross profits?" – all I got in return was a blank stare. So I asked if he knew what his gross profit per job was. He reluctantly said he did not because he did not track job costs. He had no clue how much money he was making or losing, just as long as there was cash in the bank at the end of the month. It reminded me of the joke: "I lose money on every deal, but I make it up in volume..." Do the math – it will save you a lot of time and money.

CHAPTER 33

CASH IS KING...

In God We Trust; All Others Pay Cash
~ Book by Jean Shepherd, 1966

The age of debt financing is over. Credit card companies have removed trillions of dollars from the credit market. Personal consumption accounted for seventy percent of the gross domestic product (GDP) in 2006[1]. A crippling percentage of that was financed with credit cards and home equity, so the house of cards collapsed. If you have not learned how to run your business on cash and still rely on debt financing, you will probably be a casualty of the business climate. It is time to refocus on cash.

Why is cash flow so important? It is the life blood of your company. Cash flow does not equal revenue. Cash flow does not equal profits. Cash flow does not mean the amount of money you have left in your checking account at the end of the month. Cash flow is a moving number based on sales, deposits, accounts receivable, and accounts payable. Now combine these with projected sales and expenses and you get a cash flow projection. Cash flow projecting is as much of an art as it is a science due to all of the variables, but you have to do it if you want your business to be successful and grow.

Unfortunately, most small businesses have cash flow problems. There are tens of thousands of books written about cash flow and I would

1   http://www.hoover.org/research/factsonpolicy/facts/4931661.html, May 2009.

suspect most of them are incredibly boring. This is probably one of the many reasons most business owners never read them. Who has the time and patience? So being the kumbaya kind of guy that I am, I am going to give you a crash course in cash flow management in two sentences:

1. Don't spend more than your net profits.
2. Have a reserve of cash to get you through the cash gap that occurs from the time you purchase a product for resale (or the goods to manufacture) to the time you receive the income from the sale of the product.

This may sound overly simple but I have met with more business owners than I can count who do not understand *or* follow these principles.

Here are some of the typical reasons I have found for businesses falling into a cash-flow crunch:

- The owner did not start the business with enough cash reserves.
- The business cannot survive the cash gap between paying for a product to sell and collecting payment once it is sold.
- There is not enough gross profit in each sale.
- The owner does not understand the numbers in their business and/or does not pay attention to them.
- Sales are too low to cover expenses.
- Expenses like overhead and/or payroll are too high.
- The owner did not plan for expenses like taxes or the breakdown of equipment.
- The owner is pulling more money out of the business than they should be.

So, let's do some simple math to help you figure out a thirty-day cash flow forecast to see how much cash you should have at the end of the month.

A = Starting cash

B = Cash sales for the month

C = Accounts receivable collected for the month

D = Total accounts payable and payroll due to be paid during the month

A + B + C - D = Projected cash at the end of the month

Now let's put some numbers into the formula.

A = $10.00
B = $15.00
C = $5.00
D = $12.00
$10 + $15 + $5 − $12 = $18

Eighteen dollars is the new projected cash position for the end of the next month. You can then extend this into a ninety-day forecast but it starts getting pretty complicated. Accountants can create spreadsheets from Hell to calculate cash flow, so this is a real simplistic formula; but it is a start.

Moral of the story? Fall back in love with cash. That is what keeps your business running.

CHAPTER 34

HOW MUCH RUNWAY DO YOU HAVE LEFT?

When I asked my accountant if anything could get me out of this mess I am in now, he thought for a long time and said, "Yes, death would help."
~ Robert Morley

This section is for those who are worried about their business staying open. I meet with lots of business owners whose businesses are in bad shape. Unfortunately, most people wait until they have three wheels in the ditch before they ask for help. After hearing the litany of problems: no cash, high debt, slow sales, etc., I ask, "How much runway do you have left?" In other words, if your business is a plane and cash is the runway, how long is your runway and when does it run out before you crash and burn?

It continues to amaze me how many people have not done the math and figured out how long they have until they crash. They just keep going further into debt, hoping their company will magically turn around. My experience has shown that most people don't want to do this exercise because they do not want to know the answer. Denial is a powerful emotion.

To calculate your burn rate, use the cash-flow formula in the previous section. Note that this number does not include your liabilities such as credit lines and other debt. You factor these numbers in to see if your company is still viable.

Get honest with yourself and do the math. The math will not lie to you. You will lie to yourself, but the math will not.

CHAPTER 35

OKAY, MR. JOHN D. ROCKEFELLER...
NOW WHAT DO I DO?

A budget tells us what we can't afford, but it doesn't keep us from buying it.
~ William Feather

Get profitable now. This section is for those with businesses that are in trouble – which is probably most of us.

First question on the table is what is your *immediate* goal? Keep your doors open? Increase sales? Increase cash flow? It is very important to be brutally honest about your current circumstances. Once you do that, you can make better decisions with less emotion.

Whatever your goal, the best place to start is to get profitable now with the *existing* level of revenue, not what you think the revenue *could* be. If that is not possible, what do you need to change to get there? You need to change something because what you are doing now is not working. So where to start?

- Raise prices by ten percent. For most businesses, most people will not even know the difference.
- Do job cost analysis on each product, service, and customer. **Product:** One of the biggest surprises for business owners when they first do this analysis is the discovery that what they thought was their most profitable product, turns out to be one of the least profitable. I had one client who was having financial problems and we discovered that his primary product was losing money on just about every sale. It was

difficult to see because the time between sale and payment was so long (the government was involved…) and they were not tracking it. Purchase price of the product is not the only component you need to factor into the analysis. How much support does it require? How often does it break? What about shipping?

Service: Service is one of the least-tracked expenses that I see with a lot of businesses. For example, how much payroll does it cost to produce or service an account? Service expenses can silently eat up cash.

Customer: I met with the consulting team of a client of mine to look at the profitability of each account. The consultant who worked on their biggest account said, out loud, that he knew they were losing money at the account but that "we should not raise our rates because we would lose the client." I am not making this up – he actually said this and did not even realize the folly of his remark. My suggestion was for the consultant to give the account the name of their competitor so they could help the competitor go out of business.

- Liquidate inventory. Many businesses have too much cash tied up in inventory. I have a simple rule: if the inventory is collecting dust, sell it – at cost, if necessary. If you could magically turn the inventory in your warehouse into cash, would you let it sit there on a shelf and collect dust? Of course not, but that basically is what you are doing with slow-turning inventory. Use the cash to buy products that are actually selling.

- Cut expenses. Start with ten percent. You will be amazed where you can cut costs when you HAVE to. Renegotiate your lease, communication costs, and vendor terms.

- Hit A/R hard. Stop being the bank for other companies. Implement a formal process for collections. The squeaky wheel does get the grease. I have had people tell me that they did not want to anger their customers by asking them for the money they are owed. *Huh?*

- Reduce owner income. I often find the business owner has a certain "standard of living" they would like to maintain.

When times are tough, it is time to adjust your standard of living.

- Cut payroll. For most business owners, payroll is their biggest expense. Here are some examples for cutting payroll:

  Upgrade employees. In a difficult business climate, you can probably get a better employee for less money.

  Eliminate positions. When cutting payroll, make sure you are not cutting a revenue-generating position first. I was working with an auto repair and tire center that was suffering from a severe cash-flow problem. Prior to my working with them, they had let go a minimum-wage employee who did the oil changes. When we looked harder at the outcome of that decision, we found that higher-paid mechanics were now being pulled off of higher paying and more-profitable jobs to change oil. This was actually causing the company to lose more money. We immediately rehired a minimum-wage employee to change oil.

  Cut payroll across the board. Make sure that the pain is shared equally and that the management team leads by example. The worst thing you can do as the leader of the company is to cut payroll and publicly maintain your lifestyle. If you are going to cut payroll and positions – make the cut deep and quick. Do not slowly eliminate positions or slowly cut salaries. This only breeds fear amongst the staff because they are just waiting for their turn to be the target.

Leverage technology

An unbelievable number of small-business owners are technology illiterate. They still throw bodies at a problem when technology will solve the problem quicker and cheaper. I guess they are just reluctant to give up all these manual systems they created. Another thing, having a Yahoo! email address for your business does not make you tech savvy. It only makes you look small.

Technology should be viewed like electricity and telephones: as absolute necessities – not nice-to-haves. Yet, business owners consistently try to scrimp on maintaining systems or leveraging new technologies. Would you scrimp on your electricity?

With the price of computers and accounting software these days, there is no excuse for not having an in-house computer accounting system. Again, it still amazes me how many businesses just send their "stuff" to their accountant and continue to run their business blindly. The next big mistake I see way too often is the company actually has an accounting program but the data is not accurate – and yet they keep using it. What is the point of doing that? It is not going to magically fix itself by putting more bad data into it. If you are trying to do the books yourself and your data is not accurate, hire a part-time bookkeeper. If you have a bookkeeper or accountant and your data is still inaccurate – fire them. Just because some people say they are accountants does not mean they know what they are doing. Most small businesses can get along just fine with a part-time bookkeeper, and there is no shortage of competent bookkeepers in the marketplace these days. One other thing, learn Excel. A spreadsheet can be a business owner's best friend.

I am not going to tell you to go take an accounting class. For most entrepreneurs, given the choice of taking an accounting class or slamming their thumb in a car door, they would take the car door. Therefore, hire a competent bookkeeper who can give you the numbers you need to run your business. The life of your business depends on it.

Once you have accurate data, you can be decisive and start making the hard decisions. Doing nothing is probably the worst thing you can do. Hoping it will get better does not work, either. Looking for a magic formula or "secret" that will suddenly turn your business around does not work. It is a simple equation of dollars and cents. It either works or doesn't. So pull the emotion out of the decision-making process – emotion only makes matters worse. The bottom line is – you have to know the numbers of your business – do the math (or go broke)!

EPILOGUE

*If all printers were determined not to print anything till they were sure
it would offend nobody, there would be very little printed.*
~ Benjamin Franklin

The biggest reason for business failures in this country is ignorance. Ignorance of sound business practices and ignorance of your own strengths and weaknesses. Running a small business is very hard, but it does not have to be as difficult as some business owners try to make it. The best thing some business owners can do is get out of business – if they are just not cut out for it. The best thing others can do is get out of their own way, stop being a control freak and trying to do everything, hire good employees and fire the bad ones. And understand that your leadership skills will make, or break, your business.

I realize that I probably pissed off a lot a people with this treatise. Somewhere in California I harshed somebody's mellow by my rude and insensitive comments. But the truth be told, I really don't care. I wrote this for those with common sense, who are looking for real-world solutions to their problems. If by reading this, some struggling business owner decides to change before going broke, I will consider this book a raging success. For some, the message in this book will ring true. I know I am not the only one who thinks this way.

JUST FED UP...

I did not start to write THIS book. What I thought was my main motivation led to another discovery – I'm also very fed up – fed up with the ever-increasing number of obstacles being put in front of business owners. Hey, Washington, just leave us alone and mind your own business. So, please allow me to vent while I have this soap box...

I am fed up with politicians – who have never run a business – making laws about business. Since when was minimum wage something you were supposed to raise a family of four on? Tax profits and that will make prices go down? What planet do they live on? Oh, yeah, some faraway planet called Washington D.C...

I am fed up with politicians that force small business owners to keep a job open for an employee, male or female, so they can have maternity leave. Since when was that the responsibility of the business owner? It should not be the responsibility of the business owner to provide paid time off for maternity leave so the mother can "bond" with her baby. If the business owner wants to offer that benefit, that is fine. But they should not be forced to by the government. If a woman decides to have a baby, then it should be her responsibility to suffer the economic consequences of her decision. Not her employer. And don't get me started on paid leave so the father can bond... Too late...

I pulled this off of a "parent's network" website in California. (http://parents.berkeley.edu/recommend/insurance/maternity.html, accessed July 2008)

> *My husband is having problems using Paid Family Leave for bonding with our infant son. Specifically, he wants to take intermittent leave (taking every Monday as a family leave day until he runs out of leave)... But now his employer says "intermittent" means two chunks of time, so they won't let him take Mondays off. They want him to take the rest of his leave in one big chunk (He has already taken a few days, which they consider the first chunk)...*

Here are some of the responses:

> *I am taking intermittent leave, 3 days/week until my time runs out. My understanding is that you are entitled to take the leave in any manner you see fit....*

> *I don't know exactly, but I feel your pain! We had an almost identical situation with my husband (wanting partial time off), and although his employer allowed it, they denied his request for vacation because of this "partial time" use of FMLA...*

> *I need to take care of my mother with dementia, who requires ongoing care. Can I take leave a few hours at a time? Do I have to satisfy the seven-day waiting period each time I take leave?*

Huh? Three days a week? Take a few hours at a time? The husband wants partial time off AND vacation? And the big bad business owner said "No"? The fact that somebody thought that was unreasonable on the part of the business owner scares me to death. What the hell has happened to common sense? The purpose of a business is to make a profit first. Without profit, there is no business – unless you are in the government. Only in government do laws like this make sense.

I am fed up with poor customer service.

I am fed up with employees who don't give a damn.

I am fed up with business owners losing their business because they can't get out of their own way.

I am fed up with watching too many ill-equipped business owners spend their life savings on a business, only to wind up bankrupt and depressed.

I am fed up with honest business people being put out of business because of frivolous lawsuits.

I am fed up with the notion that small businesses are an endless source of revenue (i.e., IRS, Congress, employees). Most are just barely making it.

I am fed up with employees thinking that health insurance is the responsibility of the employer. Why not car insurance? Why not homeowner's insurance, while we are at it? Where do we stop?

I am fed up with stupid people.

I am fed up with the current culture of condemning those who point out the stupidity in today's society. I saw the following on a T-shirt a little girl was wearing: "I'm not mean; you're just a sissy..." If this book makes you mad, that saying pretty much describes my sentiment about the email you might contemplate sending me.

I am fed up with motivational books that actually do nothing to change behaviors. If you are looking for some New Age metaphysical solution to succeeding in business, go read *The Secret*. Books like *The Secret* are one of the reasons I wrote this book. I actually did not read the book; I watched the video. Yes, I was one of the lemmings that ran off that cliff... *The Secret* is brilliant marketing. You mean all I have to do is "think" that my bills will disappear and they will? And I won't be that loser in the video anymore? *Cool!* And all I have to do is tap into something at the quantum physics level and I can have anything I imagine? *Really Cool!* So... just how do I go about finding something at the quantum physics level, anyway? I missed that part on the video. To be honest, they lost me when they said that if I have cancer, all I have to do is "think" it away. Why didn't I think of that? I had a friend die of lung and brain cancer and I know he watched the video. What happened? He did not "think" hard enough? This kind of stuff really pisses me off.

I am fed up with chasing the Holy Grail of business books that would give me the answers I seek – only to find theories that don't work because they are impossible to apply to the real world or are designed for billion-dollar companies.

I am fed up with political correctness. If Western culture ever collapses, it will be because of political correctness. I just hope that we are not seeing *Atlas Shrugged* coming true before our very eyes... Who is John

Galt? He is the American entrepreneur who is getting hammered from every direction. At what point do the producers in society just say, "The hell with it…"

Most of all, *I am fed up* with the dearth of common sense. I hope you were able to find some in these words. The good news is that more and more people are fed up, too, and are starting to speak up and push back. Light at the end of the tunnel? Or just a train? Only time will tell…

Ahhh… that felt good.

ABOUT THE AUTHOR

Kevin Hanville is the founder and CEO of Quadrant Group, a consulting firm that offers business transformation services across the country, focusing on increasing sales and profits and training business owners to become more effective leaders. Hanville and his team have helped hundreds of companies improve their organizational operations, saved companies from bankruptcy, and assisted others in achieving double-digit growth.

An award-winning business consultant and sales achiever, Hanville uses a direct approach and no-nonsense style that appeals to business owners. Thousands have come away from his seminars and engagements with a fresh perspective on how to make positive changes within their organizations. If you would like Kevin Hanville to address your organization, please contact Barbara Hanville at bhanville@quadrantgroup.biz or 770.277.2212 for more information.

To learn more or sign up for Kevin's free newsletter, visit www.quadrantgroup.biz or email info@quadrantgroup.biz.